GARDENS

of

ENGLAND SCOTLAND AND WALES
A GUIDE AND GAZETTEER

GARDENS

of

ENGLAND SCOTLAND AND WALES
A GUIDE AND GAZETTEER

HAZEL EVANS

GEORGE
PHILIP

Published in 1991 by George Philip Limited,
59 Grosvenor Street, London W1X 9DA

British Library Cataloguing in Publication Data

Evans, Hazel, *1928–*
    Gardens of England, Scotland and Wales.
    1. Great Britain. Gardens. Visitors' guides
    I. Title
    914.104859
    ISBN 0-540-01222-X

Page design Janette Widdows
Typeset by BAS Printers Limited,
Over Wallop, Hampshire, Great Britain
Printed in Hong Kong

———◆———

Title-page illustration *Looking across one of the lakes at Savill Garden in Surrey*

Contents

◆

Introduction

◆

It is not until we travel abroad that we come to realize fully what an immense wealth of gardens we have in Britain. And how lucky we are that so many owners are willing to share them with us. Organizations like the National Trust and the National Trust for Scotland also do vital work in ensuring that this living history is preserved for us all to enjoy.

A selection of gardens like this is, to some extent, an idiosyncratic one because of the confines of space, and while aiming to show examples of all that is best in British gardening, it is only natural that some of my own personal favourites have been included which will, I hope, become yours too.

The book is organized in the following way:

Origins A brief 16-part history, tracing the development of British gardening through the ages, from its earliest beginnings and the first known gardens made in Roman times, up to the present day. Individual sections examine, for example, the development of the herbaceous border, lawn and cottage garden, and the fascinating stories of the landscape designers and famous plant hunters and pioneers are also recounted.

Gazetteer An alphabetical list of 100 gardens in England, Scotland and Wales, which have been selected for their historical interest, originality, charm or sheer beauty.

Maps Each of the gardens described in the gazetteer is marked in red on one or more of the four preceding regional maps. In addition, six of the entries have been specially chosen to feature as a 'Guided Tour', receiving a more detailed description; these six gardens are located on the maps with red capital letters.

Glossary A concise explanation of gardening terms.

To assist the would-be visitor, practical information is also given concerning opening times, and there is a comprehensive index.

◆

Left *Stone steps decorated with ornamental urns at Acorn Bank Garden*

I
Origins

———◆———

The first known gardens in Britain were made by the invading Romans who built them in the atriums of their brand-new villas. Before the Roman period, ground was used only for growing essential crops. The Romans brought with them many plants, including lavender and other Mediterranean herbs, and even grape vines which appeared to flourish in southern England at that time.

When the Romans left it was the turn of the monks to become the nation's gardeners. Most of the plants that they grew were purely practical, and were used either for culinary or medicinal purposes or as dyes. The rich and the powerful, living in their castles, restricted their gardening activities to flowery meads, rose arbours, little fountains and plots of fragrant flowers – an antidote to the unsanitary and uncomfortable life within castle walls during the summer months of the year. When windows, if any, were little more than arrow slits, the wish to escape into the courtyard or outside the walls must have been overwhelming.

The 16th century saw the development of the large country house, such as Bess of Hardwick's HARDWICK HALL (Derbyshire); even castles built at that time were more domestic in their design, and the pleasure garden began to make its appearance. This was no longer just a place to escape for some fresh air, but somewhere to linger. Although still protected by moats, the gardens were formal in their layout, with knots of herbs and flowers. The patterns of these knots were often copied from the ornate plaster ceilings indoors.

Fountains and water features were widely used in the early 17th century. The maze or labyrinth became popular, as did the bowling green, the archery lawn and other garden games. Increasing affluence brought with it an interest in cultivating more exotic plants and fruit growing became a fashionable pastime. You will still see fireplaces in the walls of some old kitchen gardens, such as at PARNHAM HOUSE (Dorset), for example, which provided heat from stoves to warm the walls and help nectarines, peaches or apricots to ripen, and which were used right up to the 19th century. The Jacobeans and Stuarts brought gardening to a fine art, and as wealth spread downwards, smaller country house owners and cottagers began to take an interest in gardening, too.

Formal gardening in the grand manner reached its peak later in the 17th

Left Purple irises beside the lake at Sheffield Park, with autumnal trees in the distance

century, when more and more of the aristocracy travelled abroad and brought back influences and ideas not just for architecture but also for gardens and garden ornaments. Only fragments of gardens from this period in England remain. Italy and France were the main sources of inspiration at this time, in particular the gardens of the Sun King, Louis XIV, at Versailles and Fontainebleau. The French landscape designer and gardener André Le Nôtre had created the famous formal garden at Vaux-le-Vicomte in 1661 and went on to mastermind Versailles. For 100 years after this, his style was copied throughout Europe, and his influence can be seen at MELBOURNE HALL (Derbyshire) and HAMPTON COURT PALACE (London). Topiary, which dated back to Roman times, became suddenly fashionable again, but on a much more opulent scale, as at LEVENS HALL (Cumbria), and the little Elizabethan knots were made into larger, more ambitious *grands parterres* such as the one at HAMPTON COURT PALACE. Water was used lavishly and in a similar way, the water parterres being, if anything, even more elaborate than the planted ones.

By the 18th century, people had grown tired of formality carried to extremes and were looking for something less structured. CLAREMONT (Surrey) is the earliest existing example of this 'new look', begun by Sir John Vanbrugh in 1720. This was the period of the 'Grand Tour', when young gentlemen were sent around Europe to study its art and culture. The painter William Kent came back from Italy full of ideas for a more 'natural' landscape. His patron, Lord Burlington, set him to work on the gardens of his villa at CHISWICK (London) and unwittingly triggered off a gardening revolution. In 1740 Kent began work on a new garden at STOWE (Buckinghamshire), where he met a young man who was to become head gardener there: Lancelot (later nicknamed 'Capability') Brown. Between them, these men changed the face of gardening in Britain. The parterres and formal gardens were swept away, rivers were dammed, and whole villages uprooted in the cause of naturalism. The garden became a park, right up to the very walls of the house, and so popular did this landscape style of gardening become in both Britain and the rest of Europe that very few earlier gardens remain. Sad as this is for the garden historian, one good effect was the introduction of low-maintenance gardening, for the formal beds had been extremely labour-intensive. LUTON HOO (Bedfordshire), BOWOOD HOUSE (Wiltshire) and SHEFFIELD PARK (East Sussex) are some of the many examples of the landscaped garden that remain from this period.

Once again there was a reaction, and the Victorians, spurning the natural look, began to reinstate the formal garden with cheap labour. Flamboyant mansions and huge elaborate gardens were built for the rich in the 19th century, such as those at BIDDULPH GRANGE (Staffordshire), PENRHYN CASTLE (Gwynedd) and HEVER CASTLE (Kent), but so too were villas for the prosperous middle class. Smaller gardens proliferated and the first large-circulation gardening magazines

TUNNEL AT BIDDULPH GRANGE

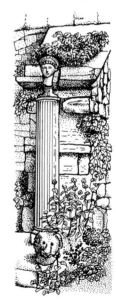

POMPEIAN WALL AT HEVER

OTHER HISTORICAL GARDENS
To get a true picture of gardening through the ages, start your odyssey at the garden of the Roman Palace at Fishbourne, near Chichester (West Sussex), then study the monastery garden at Newstead Abbey (Nottinghamshire) and the Elizabethan New Place at Stratford-upon-Avon (Warwickshire). The garden at Ham House (London) is a good example of Stuart times.

APOTHECARY'S ROSE

LILY-OF-THE-VALLEY

were published. In the country, farm workers managed their own cottage gardens and often had allotments as well. The desire for newer, bigger and better plants became an obsession towards the turn of the century as plant hunters such as E.H. Wilson and George Forrest added to the plants already introduced by Sir Joseph Banks and others, leading to gardens such as LEONARDSLEE (West Sussex), with its rhododendrons and camellias, and DYFFRYN BOTANIC GARDEN (South Glamorgan).

The beginning of the 20th century saw a return to the natural look in gardening, under the influence of first William Robinson and then Gertrude Jekyll, with gardens such as NYMANS (West Sussex). The idea of the garden as an outdoor room took hold, first at HIDCOTE MANOR (Gloucestershire), then at SISSINGHURST CASTLE (Kent), and remains just as valid today. As plots become smaller, and cities more crowded, we appreciate all the more the vision of a precious piece of greenery, a personal space outside.

THE MIDDLE AGES

After the Romans left, the appreciation of flowers seems to have died out and was not revived until the 16th century. The domestic garden, where it existed, was a sheltered place in which to sit in summer, with a turf bank, perhaps a rose bower with some scented plants, or a flowery mead, the precursor of today's lawn, as well as being somewhere to provide a few vegetables, herbs and fruit. Herbs were used for medicinal and culinary purposes as well as for dyes. We know roses existed at this time as they became emblems in the Wars of the Roses, which began in 1455 – the red rose of Lancaster was *Rosa gallica* (the Apothecary's rose, used for medicinal purposes), while the white rose of York is thought to have been *Rosa × alba* (or possibly the white dog rose, *Rosa canina*).

It is known from old manuscripts that daffodils, hollyhocks, honeysuckle, primroses, lavender and Madonna lilies were grown, together with cowslips, foxgloves, adder's tongue (*Ophioglossum*) and wood avens (*Geum urbanum*), which, together with herb Robert and plantain, grow now in the wild. But in an unlawful countryside where private armies roamed, stealing and damaging property, the urge to survive was probably stronger than that to garden.

The only contemporary account of a garden that remains is a Crown Commissioner's report on Thornbury Castle, whose owner, Edward, Duke of Buckingham, had just been executed for treason. It describes a 'proper' garden with a 'large and goodly orchard full of newly grafted fruit trees . . . many roses and other pleasures, and goodly alleys with resting-places covered thoroughly with whitethorn and hazel.' The garden was laid out by Buckingham in 1520.

The herb garden near the ruined castle at Scotney

Serious gardening, strictly for practical purposes, was carried on behind monastery walls. It is difficult today to comprehend the power of the monasteries in the Middle Ages, a reign that ended abruptly in Henry VIII's time with their dissolution. To the ordinary people, the monastery was not only a seat of learning but also a place to turn to for help when sick. With religion playing a much larger part in daily life than it does today, monasteries also provided hope of life in the hereafter and comfort in times of distress. Life in the monasteries must have been comparatively comfortable as they were rich and powerful: the monks had good food and wine, were relatively free from attack, and had the opportunity to learn to read and copy the beautiful illuminated manuscripts. But while the monks grew fat, the country people around them often lived in poverty at near starvation level.

The monasteries were largely self-sufficient. Any excess fruit and vegetables could be bartered for meat (if they did not keep their own livestock), spices and clothing; any left-overs went to the poor. They also grew dye-plants such as madder (from which the manuscript inks were made), and some monasteries grew flax from which to make linen. Their orchards often doubled as cemeteries, with the monks' graves under the fruit trees.

Monastery gardens were usually enclosed, often within cloisters, and had stout walls to keep out thieves and protect the crops from deer, rabbits and other animals which might plunder them. Tender plants would have been protected from high winds by simple wattle fencing. It is believed the monks grew some flowers, possibly to decorate the altars, and many old-fashioned plants named after Our Lady, the Virgin Mary, were probably grown mainly in monasteries. The violet was known as 'Our Lady's modesty', the cowslip 'Our Lady's lace', and the lily-of-the-valley was 'Our Lady's tears'. Roses, too, have always been associated with the Virgin Mary and it is likely that they also had a place in a monastery garden – sometimes, like the Apothecary's rose, for medicinal reasons.

The monk-gardener, or *gardinarius*, grew basic vegetables such as onions, leeks, celery, radishes, shallots, cabbages and parsnips. Culinary herbs grown and used in those days included coriander, dill, garlic, parsley, fennel and chervil. These would have been used rather lavishly in winter to disguise the all-too-strong flavour of meat or fish that had been salted and stored for some months. The brewer monk would also have a plot, growing such plants as yarrow, elder, alecost and mugwort, for making ales and herbal wines. Many monasteries in the south of England – the manors of Northfleet and Teynham in Kent, for instance – had vineyards too, and one is recorded at Peterborough, Cambridgeshire, as producing 'ver juice' for cooking. But in Norman times at least there was a plentiful supply of wine from France. Beaulieu Abbey in Hampshire was renowned for the cider from its apple orchards, and most monastery gardens also had a 'stew pond' or series of ponds in which fish such as carp, roach and bream were kept until they were needed for the pot.

The herbarium, the medicinal or physic garden under the direction of the infirmer, would be planted with all the herbs we commonly use today, but included others such as the bitter rue (grown for its attractive blue-green foliage today) and yarrow, which was used to stop bleeding. Some of these physic gardens were of a large size – the Great Infirmary Garden at Westminster Abbey, for instance, was almost 1 acre (0.4 ha) in extent. The medicinal herbs known to be used in medicine in Anglo-Saxon times and which survive in herb gardens today include southernwood, lemon balm and comfrey. It was in the herb garden that the bee-hives were placed to produce beeswax for the church candles and honey – and mead – for the monks. People needing medical care would wait to be treated at the monastery gates. They would be given agrimony for stomach pains and bistort for ulcers, while salves made from thyme or marjoram mixed with animal fat were used to treat rheumatism. The monks would also have fed and tended pilgrims on their way on foot from one holy shrine to another.

Herbs were also used for other things. A mixture of dried pennyroyal, rue and wormwood was brushed over the flagstone floors of churches to stop the spread of the many infectious diseases around in those times.

◆

THE TUDORS

Henry VIII certainly appreciated gardens as pleasure grounds – particularly for archery and bowls. With his courtiers, he set about appropriating the estates of many of the religious orders and of the clergy who fell out of favour. He took over the magnificent HAMPTON COURT PALACE (London), for example; built originally for Cardinal Wolsey, it became one of Henry's favourite homes.

Sir Thomas More, a contemporary of Wolsey and also fated to fall out of favour, built a house in 1520 in the country village of Chelsea, and laid out a garden there. A writer of that time described it as a place of marvellous beauty, full of lovely flowers and blossoming fruit trees with 'green meadows and wooded hills on every side'. The meadows and hills may have gone, but much of the rosemary growing in Chelsea gardens in London today is believed to have originated in Sir Thomas's garden.

Crowded city living was one of the less pleasant aspects of life in Tudor days, and it is known that there were street sellers at that time selling fragrant plants to mask unpleasant odours from the unsanitary conditions in which people lived. Lavender, carnations (then known as gilly flowers), violets, thyme and possibly basil were made into toilet waters or carried as nosegays.

OTHER HERB GARDENS
The cathedrals at Canterbury (Kent), Ely (Cambridgeshire) and Gloucester (Gloucestershire) all now have replanted herb gardens, as do the abbeys of Malmesbury (Wiltshire) and Glastonbury (Somerset). Charlecote Park (Warwickshire), where a young William Shakespeare was caught poaching, has a herb garden containing many of the flowers mentioned in his plays.

The labyrinth at Hatfield House is to be found in the knot garden

The *nouveau riche* members of Henry's court lost no time in building themselves fine country estates to get away from the busy, unhygienic towns of the time. Little were they to realize that they had made a rod for their own backs. Many a stately home can now claim 'Queen Elizabeth slept here', for Henry's daughter, Elizabeth I, enjoyed country visits, and when, later, she turned up, accompanied by hundreds of courtiers, she and her entourage had to be accommodated by the unfortunate owners. There were even complaints about the owners having to camp out in damp meadows to make room for the Queen.

None of the gardens of the new fine houses now exist, but Thomas Platter, who visited Nonsuch, another of the King's palaces, in Surrey, described a bowling green, a tennis court, a maze with hedges thick and high enough to prevent cheating and, in the pleasure gardens, imitation animals 'artfully set out so that one might mistake them for real ones'. Ornament certainly played an important part in Tudor pleasure gardens, probably as a result of the fashion for Italianate design which had recently arrived in England via the court of France. Paul Hentzner, a traveller to England at the end of the 16th century, described the ornaments in the garden at Theobalds in Hertfordshire: 'One goes into the garden encompassed with a ditch full of water, large enough to have the pleasure of going in a boat, and rowing between shrubs . . . labyrinths made with a great deal of labour; a *jet d'eau* with its basin of white marble; and columns and pyramids of wood up and down the garden.' He also described a summerhouse with 'twelve Roman emperors in white marble'.

Plants were being studied more scientifically now. In 1545 the first botanical garden was laid out at the University of Padua; and in England William Turner, known now as the father of English botany, who curiously enough gardened near Kew in London, produced a book giving the names of herbs in Greek, Latin, English, Dutch and French.

The rich merchants may not have been able to afford large estates, but they had gardens around their houses. Seedsmen and horticulturists sprang up in the cities. In the 1540s the brother-in-law of Sabine Saunders, wife of a merchant in Northamptonshire, recorded having bought 'seeds for my sister's new gardens'. Garden pests were in evidence too, for Thomas Hill of London produced a treatise on 'what remedies may be had and used against such beasts, worms, flies and suchlike that annoy gardens'.

Hundreds of plants are mentioned in Shakespeare's plays, commemorated not only in the SHAKESPEARIAN GARDENS at Stratford-upon-Avon (Warwickshire), but as far afield as San Francisco in California, where there is a Shakespeare garden in the botanical park, containing every one of the plants he mentions.

At this time the Dutch were already hybridizing and breeding new varieties of plants, establishing the beginnings of the great horticultural industry they have today. The Huguenots, who arrived in England as a result of religious persecution

ELIZABETHAN KNOT DESIGN

ROSEMARY

in France, were not all silk weavers but were often gardeners, and they began to grow vegetables and flowers on a commercial scale, particularly in East Anglia. Thomas Tusser published his *Five Hundred Points of Good Husbandry* in 1577. Written in doggerel, largely with women in mind, it described women gardening on their own plots, raising herbs and flowers, and also employed on some of the large estates as 'weeder women', watering and weeding the lawns of stately homes.

In the reign of Elizabeth I, gardens were used for all kinds of outdoor activities, even balls and masques. Trade with other countries brought new and exotic fruits, and at about this time the first-ever orange trees came to England, brought by Sir Francis Carew for his estate at Beddington near Croydon, London. Both John Aubrey and John Evelyn mention having visited them. There are two stories about how the trees got there – one is that Carew imported them from Italy; the other is that Sir Walter Raleigh gave him the seeds. In winter the trees had to be covered by a 'wooden tabernacle' and kept warm by stoves. Somehow they survived. Unhappily, the garden, complete with a garden house decorated with scenes of the battle of the Armada, disappeared long ago and in their place stands the modern town of Croydon. However, copies of the original Elizabethan knot gardens still exist.

Knots now began to appear in gardens belonging to yeomen and merchants. Their patterns, though smaller, were if anything more elaborate. 'Enknotted' in dwarf box, thrift or rosemary, they sometimes took the shape of heraldic beasts, or the patterns may have been copied from lace designs.

THE COTTAGE GARDEN

Hollyhocks and sunflowers, pansies and lavender, honeysuckle and roses round the door; the cottage garden, dreamed of by generations of city-dwellers, is famous the world over and re-created in many a suburban strip. Yet its history is unknown, for while rich men's estates are well documented through the years, the poor man's plot is not. However, cottage gardens of some sort certainly did exist from Roman times, though they were probably suppressed under Norman rule, and it is likely that only fruit and vegetables were grown. Medieval cottage gardeners may well have begged plants and seeds from the local monasteries.

The Black Death of 1349 was really responsible for bringing the cottage garden as we know it into existence. Because whole communities were wiped out, labour was in short supply and those who had previously been forced to work for the local lord suddenly found they had a market value and began to work for hire. Without a free labour force, landlords were soon forced to sell some of their land to the workers – and so the cottager (or cottar) came into being.

OTHER ELIZABETHAN GARDENS

The moated Elizabethan garden at Helmingham Hall, near Stowmarket (Suffolk) is well worth a visit. Cranborne Manor, near Wimborne St Giles (Dorset) has a very attractive Elizabethan knot garden filled with flowers of the time, such as pinks and crown imperials. The original Elizabethan outline can still be seen in the gardens at Montacute House, near Yeovil (Somerset), but the planting is relatively modern.

The countryman would also have a plot of communal land where he grew beans, wheat, barley or rye for his own use and for barter or sale.

Documents show that cottage life was well established by Elizabethan times, and a writer in the 1600s reports: 'There is scarce a cottage in most of the southern parts of England but has its proportionable garden, so great a delight do most men take of it.' However, it was sometimes more practical than pretty. Nearly 300 years later, Mrs Gaskell described one as containing 'a few berry bushes, space for potatoes, onions and cabbages as well as the odd herb, with a rose tree and marigolds to flavour the salt beef broth.'

Cottage garden design evolved naturally. With little space to play with, everything was crammed in: vegetables were jumbled up among flowers such as rosemary, pinks, primroses, marigolds and Madonna lilies (first grown by the monasteries as strewing herbs or for medicinal purposes), and of course the sentimental ones like mignonette and forget-me-nots. Although herbs are now seen as an essential part of the cottage garden, in early times they were grown mainly on the large estates where they were used to disguise the strong flavours of long-stored meat – a luxury unknown to the cottager. The mainstay of the cottager's diet was vegetables so this is what he grew, together with a few herbs for medicinal use. Not an inch of soil was wasted, as space was made for a clutch of cabbages, a row of onions, gooseberry bushes or currants. The cottage garden was usually sited in front of the house and had no lawn but a path between the overflowing beds. Some of the flowers in the garden had a romantic history and were brought to Britain by returning Crusaders – the turk's cap lily (*Lilium martagon*) for instance, and the Apothecary's rose (*Rosa gallica*).

Fashions in garden design came and went, leaving the cottage garden more or less untouched – although the 17th-century craze for topiary filtered down to the small plot, and fanciful animal shapes appeared in front gardens, together with edgings of carefully clipped box.

'I have learned much from the little cottage gardens that help to make our English waysides the prettiest in the temperate world,' wrote Gertrude Jekyll. 'One can hardly go into the smallest cottage garden without learning or observing something new.' And she freely admitted that she based many of her ideas for the 'natural' herbaceous border on cottage themes.

However, there was also a darker side to the idyllic scene. 'Among the things made by man, nothing is prettier than an English cottage garden,' wrote William Robinson at the end of the 19th century, but this picture-postcard ideal exemplified in countless genteel watercolours of thatched cottages, hollyhocks and sunbonnets hid the real facts. Crammed into cities after the Industrial Revolution, people dreamed – as they do today – of an ideal life in the country. But the reality was far from ideal for most country people. Successive Acts of Enclosure, from 1845 onwards, took common land away from agricultural workers so they were

FORGET-ME-NOT

Left *The terrace garden at East Lambrook Manor*

no longer able to grow crops for their own use or to sell. As a result, the cottage plot became even more important as a working garden. Even the flowers had to earn their keep, and were grown for medicinal purposes – pansies for convulsions, honeysuckle for coughs, rosemary for sore throats.

Cottage gardens of the kind that influenced Gertrude Jekyll or William Robinson were more likely to be found in parsonages. One of these belonged to Canon Ellacombe who wrote about his cyclamens and hellebores, dogtooth violets and peonies in the *Guardian* newspaper in the 1890s and started the Cottage-Gardening Society. George Eliot wrote about one such garden in *Scenes of Clerical Life*, describing a 'paradisaical mingling of all that was pleasant to the eye and good for food. The rich flower-border running along every walk, with its endless succession of spring flowers, anemones, auriculas, wall-flowers, sweet-williams, campanulas, snap-dragons, and tiger-lilies . . . .' The author Miss Mary Russell Mitford also wrote about her cottage plot full of hollyhocks, roses and honeysuckle in the *Ladies Magazine*; her column, 'Our Village', was read with avidity and envy by the ladies living in town.

It was only in this century that agricultural workers became prosperous enough to have gardens for decorative purposes rather than for survival – but by then many of them were deserting the countryside for the town. Cottage gardening in the wake of Gertrude Jekyll moved into the hands of the middle classes: Margery Fish's garden at EAST LAMBROOK MANOR (Somerset) carried on the tradition, as did Vita Sackville-West's SISSINGHURST CASTLE (Kent), and SCOTNEY CASTLE (Kent) has its own cottage garden too.

Today the cottage tradition is alive and well, and developing into a fine art. But it is no longer in the hands of the original cottagers, the agricultural workers, but of wealthier weekenders who are impassioned gardeners and fill the borders with all the old-fashioned flowers that have flourished in cottages for centuries.

HONEYSUCKLE

ANOTHER COTTAGE GARDEN
To see a modern version of the cottage garden border be sure to visit Dartington Hall (Devon), where Gertrude Jekyll's planting principles have been carried through.

GARDENING IN THE GRAND MANNER

It depends which school of thought you adhere to, whether you consider the 17th or the 18th century to be Britain's greatest period of gardening history. No one will disagree, however, that the late 17th century was certainly one of the grandest. Even the execution of Charles I and the temporary rule of the Puritans failed to halt the changes in design that were taking place.

The beginning of the 17th century saw the building of HATFIELD HOUSE (Hertfordshire), the home of Robert Cecil, Earl of Salisbury. The Jacobean mansion was begun in 1607, with the gardens started in 1609 – although they took years to complete. A vineyard was planted with 30,000 vines, and thousands

MAGNOLIA

TERRACES AT POWIS CASTLE

of trees, shrubs and herbaceous plants were imported from abroad. The Queen of France made Cecil a gift of 500 fruit trees, and gardeners were imported from France to work on the scheme.

Explorers and adventurers had been bringing plants back from their travels, and this had led to a fashionable obsession with new plants. Most were found through agents, including John Tradescant, who was later to work more closely with Lord Salisbury. There are bills in existence from that time for purchases made in Holland and in Paris. Tradescant bought, among other things, 200 cypress trees at 'one shilling the peece'. After Robert Cecil's death, Tradescant went further afield: he was buzzed by pirates off the Algerian coast, travelled to Russia, and collected plants from the New World, many of which bear his name today and can be found in the TRADESCANT GARDEN in Lambeth (London).

There was now a more academic interest in plants, and John Gerard published his famous *Herbal*, now generally accepted as being plagiarist. He took the books of a Belgian botanist of that time, Rembert Dodoens, and, with the help of Mrs Gerard, added some 'snippets for women', as he called them, passing the work off as his own. Many gardening writers emerged in this century: John Parkinson, the king's herbalist, published his book of gardening tips, *Paradisi in Sole Paradisus Terrestris*, in 1629. And John Evelyn, diarist and dilettante, crony of Charles II, wrote *Pomona*, a book on fruit trees, and *Acetaria, A Discourse of Sallets*, as well as his famous book on trees, *Sylva or Discourse on Forest Trees*, published in 1664. Evelyn's pride and joy at his Sayes Court estate, in Deptford, London (situated at that time in deep countryside), was an 'impregnable holly hedge of about four hundred foot in length, nine foot high and five in diameter' which 'I can show in my now-ruined garden'. The Tsar of Muscovy, Peter the Great, had rented Evelyn's house while in England, and had promptly wrecked the hedge by getting his courtiers to push him in and out of it in a wheelbarrow.

In the early part of the century, Francis Bacon, Viscount St Albans, gave a picture of the ideal garden, which is not all that different from ours. It should, he said, be planted so that there is something to enjoy in each of the 12 months; and it should be enjoyment in its widest sense, covering colours and scents of flowers, crops of fruit, shiny evergreen leaves in winter and the smell of herbs crushed underfoot. There should be hedges to provide shaded walks in summer, and somewhere to exercise. There should be a wild garden, but ponds with 'stagnating water' should not be permitted. However, Bacon's ideal small garden was meant to cover some 30 acres (12 ha) of ground.

In the latter part of the century the influence became entirely Continental. By now more people – certainly the nobility – were travelling, and they returned from Italy and France to build magnificent houses and gardens in imitation of those they had seen abroad. The reconstructed Italian garden at PENSHURST PLACE (Kent) dates from this time, as do the terraces of POWIS CASTLE (Powys).

Landscape designers and nurserymen were hired, sparking off thriving new industries, and everything became larger than life: the houses and the gardens, with their terraces, ornaments and water features.

In 1661, André Le Nôtre, indisputably the greatest gardener of his time, was asked by a rising – and corrupt – civil servant, Nicholas Fouquet, to create the gardens around a new château he was building at Vaux-le-Vicomte in France. The work took five years and Le Nôtre, by then in his forties, created there the first of his now-famous geometric landscapes and vistas. The gardens became such a talking point that jealous Louis XIV, the Sun King, jailed Fouquet on some pretext and commissioned Le Nôtre to design the gardens for Versailles. It took 16 years and a workforce of 36,000 men to create the mile-long canal, the huge parterres, the *allées* and the water features, but garden history was made.

Charles II, who had earlier been exiled in France, tried to entice Le Nôtre to England, but although his influence can be seen in many gardens – MELBOURNE HALL (Derbyshire), for example – he never made the trip across the Channel. Charles II ordered the royal gardens at HAMPTON COURT PALACE (London) to be transformed in the fashion of Le Nôtre, but it never really worked – writers at that time described his parterres as 'the meanest in Europe'.

Thanks to Le Nôtre, this was the century when the effects of the vista were discovered. Before then, most gardens were small, domestic and enclosed, a relic of the days of castle living. Now it became fashionable to have *allées*, or walks, radiating from the house or some other central feature, along which there would be views, often marked by an ornament in the far distance. The last idea of one's home being a fortress was swept away, and the garden began to open up, look out over and blend in with the countryside beyond. There was a craze for planting trees, fuelled by John Evelyn's famous book, and it became a fashion to plant a little 'wilderness' of forest trees somewhere on the estate, in contrast to the formality of the parterres and ornamented terraces around the house.

———————◆———————

A PASSION FOR TOPIARY

Although we usually associate topiary with 16th- and 17th-century gardens, this urge to control nature has its beginnings much further back. The word 'topiary' comes from the Latin *topiarius*, meaning an ornamental gardener, and in the days of ancient Rome, Pliny described part of his garden set out in the form of a circus 'ornamented in the middle with box cut in numberless different figures, together with a plantation of shrubs prevented by shears from shooting up too high.'

It is not known when topiary first came to Britain, but it is likely that the

Right *Looking down on to the statue of Apollo at Powis Castle*

ANOTHER GRAND GARDEN
Well worth a visit is the early 18th-century garden at St Paul's Walden Bury (Hertfordshire), birthplace of Queen Elizabeth, the Queen Mother, with its temple, statues and hedge-lined rides through woodland. The gardens were laid out in 1730 when the house was built.

idea was brought over by the conquering Roman armies. Certainly in medieval times it was the custom to train trees, bushes and climbers over frames of osiers or willow branches to make arbours and tunnels. Mazes began to appear, too, cut in turf. They were not for decoration but had a religious significance – a symbolic tortuous path for penitents to tread to righteousness; there is a maze of this kind set in the floor of Chartres Cathedral in France.

By the time of Henry VIII, little knots or frames of clipped box were used to make fanciful shapes or to edge flower beds. When Henry himself built a mount at HAMPTON COURT PALACE (London) by piling soil on a foundation of over a quarter of a million bricks, he crowned it with topiary work. Writing later in 1599, Sir Thomas Platter reported that the privy garden at HAMPTON COURT contained 'all manner of shapes, men and women, half men and half horse, sirens, serving maids with baskets . . . all true to life . . . trimmed and arranged picture-wise that their equal would be difficult to find.'

In Elizabethan times when the garden became a pleasure ground, a new form of maze, or labyrinth, became popular, with no religious significance. These were made in deliberately confusing patterns, with blind alleys, and later on hedges became taller so you could not see over them. The famous HAMPTON COURT maze was built in 1690 for Queen Anne.

Topiary finally came into its own in the 17th century, as at LEVENS HALL (Cumbria), when the fashion for garden ornament reached its height, but it was Le Nôtre who raised it to an international art form. If you look at contemporary pictures of Le Nôtre gardens, you are struck by the fact that most space is taken up by inanimate objects such as gravel, stone and wood; plants only enter as ingredients of the desired pattern – box parterres were partnered by trees and shrubs clipped into strict shapes that made them look almost unreal. The exiled Charles II was so impressed by this that he brought the ideas back to England when he returned to the throne, starting a fashion that spread all over the country. When William and Mary came to power, they added more patterns and shapes that were in vogue in the Netherlands, and built a 'fort' with crenellated walls of clipped yew and holly in Kensington Gardens. Large amounts of ready-made topiary were imported from Holland at this time, and you can still buy prepared topiary from specialist Dutch nurseries today.

One of the first things to go when the 18th-century landscape movement got under way was topiary. Alexander Pope wrote sarcastically of 'Greens to be disposed of by an eminent town-gardener' including 'Adam and Eve in Yew, Adam a little Shattered by the Tree of Knowledge in the great Storm; Eve and the Serpent very flourishing; the Tower of Babel not yet finished; St George in box, his arm scarce long enough . . . a green dragon of the same with tail of ground ivy for the present . . . and a Quick-set Hog shot up into a Porcupine, by its being forgot a Week in rainy Weather.' The essayist Joseph Addison, too,

MAZE AT HEVER CASTLE

PITMEDDEN'S TOPIARY BUTTRESSES

Right *Part of the 'Sermon on the Mount' topiary at Packwood House*

said he would rather look upon a tree 'in all its Luxuriancy and Diffusion of Boughs and Branches' than when it was 'cut and trimmed into a Mathematical Figure'. Flourishing trees were uprooted and thrown aside or else left unclipped, as happened at POWIS CASTLE (Powys). Only in one or two estates did the clipped shapes stay untouched – notably at LEVENS HALL which was, perhaps, too far from London and the centre of fashion at that time to be influenced by it. Much of the ancient topiary we see today – at PACKWOOD HOUSE (Warwickshire), for example, with its giant overcrowded 'Sermon on the Mount' – is much larger than its originators meant it to be. And the vast yew arbour at Drummond Castle in Tayside can never have been intended to reach the huge size it has today. In many gardens, now, scaffolding has to be erected before the shapes can be clipped, surely not the intention of the original designers.

With the return of more regimented gardening and geometric layouts in the 19th century, it was natural that topiary should return, spreading from the large estates through to cottage gardens. It appealed to the Victorian love of order, and labour was still cheap, so keeping bushes and hedges clipped and shapely was not a problem. Once again, topiary tended towards extremes, with such oddities as yews being turned into an Egyptian temple at BIDDULPH GRANGE (Staffordshire). But with the return to natural planting under William Robinson and Gertrude Jekyll, topiary sank once more into oblivion, although clipped hedges and pleached trees were soon to be used to make 'garden rooms' such as those at HIDCOTE MANOR (Gloucestershire) and SISSINGHURST CASTLE (Kent).

There is a resurgence of interest in topiary today, due perhaps in no small way to the invention of the electric hedge clipper which makes it possible to turn a small-leaved shrub into a pyramid or a globe in minutes.

OTHER TOPIARY GARDENS
You should visit the ancient figures cut in box, encircled by a yew hedge, at Chastleton Manor (Oxfordshire), and the wedding cakes, pyramids and spirals at Beckley Park (Oxfordshire). Haseley Court (Oxfordshire) also has an attractive topiary garden dating back to 1850. The clipped animals at Ilmington Manor (Warwickshire) are newer, being created in the 1920s.

THE ROYAL HORTICULTURAL SOCIETY

With an increasing interest in gardening, a number of special interest groups came into being in the late 18th and early 19th centuries, and with them the first garden shows – though these were small local affairs. Nothing happened nationally until a spring day in March 1804, when seven men met at Hatchard's bookshop in Piccadilly, London, for 'the purpose of instituting a society for the improvement of horticulture'. The result of that meeting is the world's best-known annual horticultural event – the Chelsea Flower Show.

John Wedgwood, the youngest and liveliest of the group, was the man who had the idea in the first place, and contacted the others. Son of the potter Josiah Wedgwood, he was a keen and knowledgeable gardener. Wedgwood had struck up a friendship with another member of the seven, William Forsyth – from whom

GARRYA ELLIPTICA

MONTEREY PINE

the plant forsythia gets its name – when Forsyth was gardener to George III and had advised Wedgwood on his garden.

The third member of the group was the Rt. Hon. Charles Greville, a collector of rare plants, and the fourth, the best known today, was Sir Joseph Banks who had accompanied Captain Cook on his first voyage to Australia. The remainder of the group consisted of two botanists and another gardener, William Aiton, who had laid out the gardens of the Royal Pavilion at Brighton.

And that was how the Horticultural Society of London, as it was then known, came into being. Its aims stated high-mindedly that: 'horticulture alone appears to have been neglected and left to the common gardener, who generally pursues the dull routine of his predecessor; and if he deviates from it, rarely possesses a sufficient share of science and information to enable him to deviate with success.'

At first the Society's work was academic and consisted of publishing a series of scientific papers by learned botanists of the day, called *Transactions*. Some of these were illustrated by colour engravings, and those by the artist William Hooker are much-prized masterpieces today. Members, or Fellows, were elected to the Society, which was granted a charter in 1809 as a learned scientific body. Nine years later, however, mainly due to the energy of its secretary at that time, Joseph Sabine, things began to move on the practical front. The Society opened an experimental garden in Kensington on a $1\frac{1}{2}$ acre (0.6 ha) plot, which soon proved too small, and in 1822 they moved to 33 acres (13 ha) at Chiswick.

From then on, plants rather than papers came to the fore, and Fellows began to bring unusual and interesting specimens to meetings in the Society's rooms. Soon, competitions were held, and these became so popular that in 1833 a larger show was held in Chiswick under a tent. It was turned into a social event, with a band and refreshments, and thus the first modern flower show was born.

One of the main aims of the Horticultural Society was to show new plants that had been collected overseas, and it soon began to rival KEW (London), sending collectors all over the world. David Douglas brought in a large number of new specimens from America, some of which have become common garden plants today – *Mahonia aquifolium*, *Clarkia elegans* (named after Captain William Clark of the Lewis and Clark expeditions), the wall shrub *Garrya elliptica* with its long silvery catkins, and the poached-egg plant, *Limnanthes douglasii*. Later Douglas introduced some superb conifers, the Douglas fir (*Pseudotsuga menziesii*), the Monterey pine (*Pinus radiata*) and the western red cedar (*Thuja plicata*).

In 1836 the Society, pursuing its high-minded (or snobbish) ideals decided that its gardeners must be educated; no young men were to be admitted into the garden as journeymen who had not had some school education, and they would only recommend men for situations as head gardeners who had been regularly examined in scientific knowledge and received a certificate stating their degree of proficiency. (There is no mention of women workers in the

A beautiful flower border at Wisley – the garden for gardeners

Society's papers at that time, but a little later its rival at KEW appointed the first lady gardeners. The young women worked in tweed bloomers, which looked rather like golfing plus-fours but were more practical than the voluminous skirts of the period; however, they caused a sensation and were ordered to wear long coats to cover them up.)

In 1861 the Horticultural Society received royal patronage, changed its name and moved back into London to new gardens at Kensington. These were sited near the present Royal Albert Hall and covered $22\frac{1}{2}$ acres (9 ha) in all. The gardens were liberally peppered with statues – many of them remainders from the Great Exhibition of 1851, part of which had been on the site – and surrounded by arcades in stone or brick. There were decorative 'gravel and ribbon beds', a throwback to the old parterres, designed to compensate for the lack of flowers in winter. But the new premises encouraged sightseers at the expense of real gardeners – Trollope mentions them as a tourist attraction rivalling Madame Tussaud's – and in 1882 the lease was given up. The Society's fortunes were on the wane and it was decided to move to cheaper premises and hold fortnightly shows in a drill hall at Buckingham Gate.

Membership numbers began to revive and in 1888 the Society ventured to hold another annual show, with exotic plants, refreshments and brass bands, at the Temple Gardens on the Embankment. It was a great success and was followed by others. Needing more space, the Society decided to lease the 28-acre (11 ha) grounds of the Royal Hospital at Chelsea in May 1912. The rest is history: nearly 200,000 people came to see the displays of exotic plants, topiary and, for the first time, gardening accessories and tools, and the Society has never looked back. Now, in the 1990s, numbers are so great that tickets are only issued in advance.

The Society leases the grounds from the Royal Hospital for 40 days, and erects on it the largest marquee in the world, covering $3\frac{1}{2}$ acres (1.4 ha). The run-up to the show is a frantic time for exhibitors: plants have to be 'brought on' in heated greenhouses, or slowed down in special cool rooms to be perfect for the week, while designs for stands or exhibition gardens have to be completed. The royal family always visits the show on the Monday afternoon before it is officially opened; celebrities appear and have flowers named after them; there are even stories of chicanery behind the scenes, with unscrupulous thieves stealing pollen off prize flowers with a sable paintbrush to use in clandestine hybridizing.

Nowadays gardening accessories, displays by parks departments and educational exhibits take up much of the room but the flowers are still the stars of the show. Anyone can apply to exhibit at Chelsea, and among the giants in the marquee you will find many small one-man specialist stands displaying the prized bronze, silver or gold medals – all part of Chelsea's charm.

Members of the Society today have a monthly journal, *The Garden*. There are also special cut-price tickets for Members' days, free visits to many beautiful gardens including WISLEY (Surrey) and ROSEMOOR (Devon), advice on gardening problems and, most important of all, free entry to all of the flower shows held each month in London.

◆

LANDSCAPES

The start of the 18th century saw changes in garden design that were more sweeping than any that had gone before. Under the landscape movement hedges, parterres and flowers were all removed, while walls and fences were replaced by ha-has. The garden became part of the landscape – and the landscape came into the garden. This man-made countryside was only achieved at considerable expense. Rivers were diverted or dammed (sometimes whole villages were moved), while hills were built or removed. All this involved huge numbers of labourers in the days before the invention of earth-moving machinery. The landscape movement coincided with what was to be one of the greatest periods of British architecture – the Georgian age – and the gardens to go with them were an act of faith. Neither owners nor landscape designers would live to see the true result of their labours; only mounds of newly-turned soil, clusters of young saplings, and muddy lakes gouged out of river-beds.

The man who initiated all this change was the Yorkshireman William Kent, painter, landscape gardener and architect – though more architect than gardener, as can be seen from the many 'buildings' (temples, gateways and obelisks) that he put into his plans; STOWE LANDSCAPE GARDENS (Buckinghamshire) is a good example. Kent was fortunate all his life in finding patrons. He studied first as a painter, with generous financial help, and in his thirties, while on an art tour of Italy, met Lord Burlington. Burlington, like Kent an admirer of the Palladian style of architecture, brought Kent back to England and set him to work on landscaping the gardens around his villa, CHISWICK HOUSE (London), where Kent made the first tentative steps in the direction he was later to follow to extremes.

Kent then went on to remodel the 30-acre (12 ha) estate at ROUSHAM PARK (Oxfordshire) in a 'natural' manner, cleverly building in views of the countryside beyond. But it was while he was working on STOWE, one of his most ambitious projects, that he met the young man who would eventually take his basic precepts and push them one stage further.

Lancelot Brown (later known as 'Capability' Brown – 'the garden has capabilities') was born in 1716, the son of a Northumberland farmer. As a youth he worked as a gardener locally, but moved south in his twenties to a job as a gardener at STOWE, where he met William Kent. Kent was then 56 years old, Brown a mere 24. Brown was eager to learn. As he watched STOWE take shape with its trees

Right A view over Chatsworth's west terrace garden to the park beyond

and temples, he assimilated at the same time Kent's ideals. He became head gardener at STOWE and persuaded the owner, Lord Cobham, to let him make some more improvements to the scene. He then began to design new landscapes for other places – Warwick Castle, for instance, where in 1749 he removed the small formal gardens and replaced them with lawns and groups of trees. 'The view pleased me more than I can express,' wrote Hugh Walpole after a visit. 'One sees what the prevalence of taste does. Little Brooke . . . has submitted to let his garden and park be natural.' By then Kent had died, and Lancelot Brown was ready to take over his mantle.

Brown went on to create hundreds more gardens, or 'landskips' as they were called, notably those at BLENHEIM PALACE (Oxfordshire), CHATSWORTH (Derbyshire) and SYON PARK (London). On the debit side, he did away with many beautiful formal gardens, whole estates and even villages. But on the credit side you only have to visit BLENHEIM PALACE, for instance, to see the fine landscapes he created, giving Britain, for the first time, a recognizable gardening style all its own.

'Capability' Brown's successor, Humphry Repton, spent five years studying botany, but did not take up gardening until he was in his thirties. In 1788, after a business venture foundered, he decided on the spur of the moment to set up as a landscape gardener. With the blessing of 'Capability' Brown's son, a Member of Parliament, he became an immediate success and eventually set up in partnership with the architect John Nash, who had been responsible for the terraces in Regent's Park.

Repton added another vital ingredient to the landscape ideas of Kent and Brown: practicality. Instead of placing houses 'on a naked lawn' he sited them to one side, nearer the farm, stable and other buildings that serviced them. He reintroduced the terrace and, to a limited extent, flowers. In order to achieve perfection in landscape design he believed there were four requisites: first, the design must 'display the natural beauties, and hide natural defects'; second, boundaries should be carefully disguised or hidden; third, it should look natural, no matter how much artifice was used; and finally, 'all objects of mere convenience or comfort, if incapable of being made ornamental or . . . proper parts of the general scenery, must be removed or concealed.'

There is a final ironic footnote to the landscape story: at the very beginning of the 18th century the Duchess of Beaufort imported a new flower from abroad for her Badminton garden in the Cotswolds. It was regarded with great curiosity at the time – and when the inevitable reaction to naked landscape came in the next century, bringing with it a return to formality and a super-abundance of flower power, this plant came into its own. It was the archetypal bedding plant of all time – the geranium (*Pelargonium*).

GERANIUM

OTHER LANDSCAPE GARDENS
The many splendid landscape gardens in Britain include Harewood House, near Harrogate (West Yorkshire), with its lake, fine cascade and undulating countryside; Attingham Park, near Shrewsbury (Shropshire), which was landscaped by Humphry Repton; and Sheringham Hall (Norfolk), also the work of Repton.

STATUES, TEMPLES AND FOLLIES

The urge to ornament the garden has a long and fascinating history which goes back to ancient Greece and Rome, from where the world's greatest and most copied statues come. Interest in garden decoration was first revived in the 1500s in Italy, when ancient figures were used to decorate the Pope's garden in the Vatican. Italy quickly became the inspiration, and indeed the source, for their increasing use in gardens from then on. It is known, for instance, that the Earl of Arundel took Inigo Jones to Italy in the early 1600s to gain ideas, and brought back to England a collection of fine statues which he displayed on the parterres of his house in the Strand in London, where they were much admired.

WILD BOAR AT CASTLE HOWARD

John Evelyn added to this by writing enthusiastically about statuary and its use in Italy and France. He described how statues were protected in niches covered by wooden doors in winter, a practice that was not followed in England with the result that both marble and stone deteriorated rapidly. This led to the use of lead statues, which were painted to look like marble, stone or bronze.

The sundial as a garden ornament arrived some time at the beginning of the 16th century, and was used mainly as a focal point for small herb gardens or knots. Henry VIII placed several of them in the gardens of HAMPTON COURT PALACE (London); the statuary there consisted mainly of images of the heraldic King's Beasts at this time.

Garden buildings tended at first to be practical: banqueting pavilions, not intended for banquets as we know them but for dessert after the main meal indoors, built away from the house on a hill (LONGLEAT, Wiltshire, has its banqueting pavilions on the roof); sheltered arbours covered with roses; and tall 'hunting towers' from which to watch the popular sports of hare coursing or hawking.

MONKEY AT MELBOURNE HALL

Garden decoration was at its height in the 17th century. Every self-respecting estate had to have ornaments placed strategically on terraces or parterres, or hidden among vegetation to surprise. Statues fell into two categories: classical statues with satyrs, cupids, Roman senators, slaves and sphinxes; or idealized peasant figures such as shepherd boys. There were also statues of animals such as the famous wild boar at CASTLE HOWARD (North Yorkshire), the monkeys at MELBOURNE HALL (Derbyshire), and the amusing 'sacred' cow at BIDDULPH GRANGE (Staffordshire). Statues, according to John Woolridge in 1677, were for 'Winter diversion . . . to recompense the loss of past pleasures and to buoy up hope of another Spring.'

The landscape movement, however, swept in, decided that statues were vulgar (like garden gnomes today) and instead used plainer vases and urns for adornment. These neo-classical designs often had Latin inscriptions and tended to be placed in or near the fashionable classical temple. Garden buildings were all the rage and became an integral part of garden design on a grand scale. There were imposing triumphal arches like the one at SHUGBOROUGH (Staffordshire), based on Greek

The lake at Stourhead, with temples in the far distance amid autumn trees

or Roman designs; temples like Vanbrugh's Temple of the Winds at CASTLE HOWARD, or the even more ambitious Praeneste by William Kent at ROUSHAM PARK (Oxfordshire) – a temple with seven arches. But it is at STOURHEAD (Wiltshire) and STOWE (Buckinghamshire) that the art of garden buildings reached a peak which has never been surpassed. Temples, pantheons, grottoes, obelisks, pyramids, hermitages and mock tombs were dotted around the grounds of many large estates, often designed to be focal points at the end of vistas.

When terraces became once again fashionable in the early 19th century, the fashion for statues also returned, together with balustrades and columns. In the Edwardian era, the millionaire William Waldorf Astor bought a whole balustrade from the Villa Borghese in Rome to decorate the terrace at CLIVEDEN (Berkshire), and then a large number of statues and sarcophagi for HEVER CASTLE (Kent). He was followed by fellow American William Randolph Hearst, who filled the gardens of St Donat's in South Wales with statuary.

The British like adorning their gardens, and one notable expression of British eccentricity so often commented on by foreigners lies in the architectural folly, which made its appearance from the 17th century onwards, but reached its height during the 'landscape' era. Follies came in many guises, from sham castles to ruined temples, 'druid' stone circles (Stonehenge-style) and tall towers. Castles were a favourite subject, and because they were solidly built many of their crenellated walls and ivy-covered towers remain. They were built as memorials to wives, or to friends; Lawrence Castle, near Exeter in Devon, for example, was built by Sir Robert Palk as a memorial to Major-General Lawrence. Others are even dedicated to favourite pets.

A popular conceit was a huge archway leading to nowhere, while many follies were religious in theme. Others had some practical purpose: they were observatories or dovecotes, or mock cottages built to house exotic birds. Some of the buildings at STOWE could be described as follies, notably Stowe Castle, with its forbidding battlements and towers; it is in reality the back of a farmhouse. Many follies were built in romantic 'Gothick' style with tall arched windows.

Sadly, many famous follies of the past have fallen into decay through sheer neglect. But there are hopeful signs that the fashion for fantasy and fun has returned. Demonstration gardens at recent Chelsea Flower Shows indicate that the old skills have not been lost, for several have featured convincingly 'ancient' ruins, built in the space of a week. And the folly tradition is still carried on by some of our more enlightened gardeners. Roger and John Last have transformed their country garden in southern England with 'ruined' walls (built from flint and stone), gateways that lead to nowhere, and a tower folly that looks as though it has been there for centuries, with a dead-end spiral staircase inside.

OTHER GARDENS WITH FOLLIES

Lord Lytton's folly in the deer park at Knebworth House (Hertfordshire) is a small piece of a church that he built complete with Gothic windows; it straddles a stream from which the deer drink. On a more urban note, the curious arch at Brookmans Park, near St Albans (Hertfordshire), built in the early 18th century by Sir Jeremy Sandbrooke, is said to have a farthing laid under every brick, making it by modern standards worth a great deal of money.

WATER GARDENS

Water has always been an important element in the garden. In ancient times, especially in hot climates such as those of Persia and India, it was appreciated not just for its cooling effect but was also given mystical and religious significance. Most of the ancient civilizations grew up around rivers as a source of life and for the irrigation of crops. But even from early times water was used for decoration too: the pharaohs had their lily ponds, and as far back as 2500 BC the Incas built glittering water basins from gold and silver.

When the Romans came to Britain they used water as a garden feature, for pools and fountains. But the art was lost, and in the Middle Ages water was put to more practical use, with ponds to farm fish for the table in the monasteries.

With the Renaissance in the 16th century, the art of water gardening was revived in new and decorative ways, shooting up from elaborate fountains, tumbling down water staircases, and descending in sheets from cascades. The extraordinary water garden at the Villa d'Este at Tivoli, near Rome, can still be seen today with its water organ, its avenue of a hundred fountains, cascades, waterfalls and water staircases.

It was the water garden of Renaissance Italy that inspired British landscape architects in the 17th century to produce 'waterworks' of their own. They vied with each other to produce larger and more spectacular sights: steam engines were used to throw the jets of fountains 120 ft (37 m) or more into the air; there were water parterres with stone boats 'moored' in them and other such fantasies. At HATFIELD HOUSE (Hertfordshire), Robert Cecil called in four different hydraulic engineers in turn to organize a water feature centred on a huge marble basin. From this, water flowed in an artificial winding stream (which caused enormous problems at the time), inlaid with coloured pebbles and mother-of-pearl.

At Enstone in Oxfordshire the waterworks in the garden of Thomas Bushell (built in the 1620s and 1630s) caused a Lieutenant Hammon to write: 'On the side of a hill is a rock . . . from the bottom whereof (by turning of a cock) riseth and spouts about 9 feet high a stream which raiseth on his top a silver ball. And as said stream riseth or falleth to any pitch or distance, so doth the ball, with playing tossing and keeping at the top of said ascending stream.'

The waterworks at CHATSWORTH (Derbyshire), however, remain the engineering masterpiece of 17th-century Britain. Water to service the great Cascade, built in 1696, is supplied by natural pressure from four large man-made reservoir lakes, hidden on the plateau above the wood. They, in turn, are fed from miles of conduits coming from the moor. The Cascade House and its forecourt both contain a series of fountains and jets which feed the Cascade, which is 208 yards (190 m) long. Even the dome of the Cascade House can be turned into a waterfall, and the interior floor is pierced by hidden jets designed, as the present Duchess of Devonshire says, 'to soak the surprised visitor'.

CASTLE HOWARD'S ATLAS FOUNTAIN

THE RIVER GOD AT STOURHEAD

The remarkable Cascade at Chatsworth was designed by Grillet in 1696

Surprising the visitor with aquatic jokes had become a popular aristocratic game at the beginning of the 17th century. *Giochi d'acqua* and *Wasserspiele* – jokes involving jets of water – had been a feature of Continental gardens for some time. In the gardens at Augsburg in Germany, for instance, the ladies were invited to lean over the bridge and look at the fish, when fine jets of water suddenly sprayed them: 'incontinently the petticoats and legs of the fair spectators are invaded with a refreshing coolness from these tiny water-spouts.' Statues suddenly spewed out water without warning, garden seats turned into fountains when sat upon, artificial trees started to rain . . . it was all taken in good part.

Water was used in a completely different way in the 18th century, when Kent and then 'Capability' Brown, not content to leave existing water features alone, made huge 'natural' lakes by damming rivers, and turned straight streams into meanders and others into decorative canals – the garden of BOWOOD HOUSE (Wiltshire) is a fine example. In their bare, newly-dug state, some of these waterworks came in for criticism. The acerbic Dr Johnson remarked to Boswell when they visited BLENHEIM PALACE (Oxfordshire) and viewed 'Capability' Brown's lake: 'You and I, Sir! have, I think, seen together the extremes of what can be seen in Britain: the wild rough Isle of Mull – and Blenheim Park.' Man-made lakes were, of course, not new. There is a story of how in 1591 Lord Hertford excavated a lake in the shape of a crescent moon specially for an entertainment to be given in honour of Queen Elizabeth I.

Together with the classical temples and follies that accompanied this new style of landscaping came ornately decorated grottoes, often built at the edge of a lake and usually including water in some form. Alexander Pope had one in the garden of his Thames-side villa at Twickenham, entered by a subterranean passage where the river's 'translucent wave shines a broad mirror through the shadowy cave'. STOURHEAD (Wiltshire) has a fine grotto, and one of the most beautiful examples remaining is that built at Bristol by Thomas Goldney in 1764, which took almost 30 years to complete. A torrent of water inside the grotto was worked by a steam engine, and the walls of the grotto are almost completely covered with shells.

Most grottoes were deliberately designed to look melancholy and bat-ridden. Some, however, were cosier, such as the grotto built by Lord Halifax for his mistress at HAMPTON COURT PALACE (London), which was built on the edge of a heart-shaped lake, encrusted inside with shells and glittering minerals, and is said to have contained a fireplace and a bed.

The 19th century has added more water to the garden scene, with some charming and eccentric adornments such as the corkscrew fountain at ALTON TOWERS (Staffordshire).

THE VICTORIAN GARDEN

Gardening became a universal passion in Victorian times. Almost everybody gardened in some way, from the working class with their new allotments or auriculas grown in pots on the windowsill, to the grandest country homes. This was the century that saw the start of the new gardening magazines and books, some of them, like Jane Loudon's, written especially for ladies. There was a rise in garden manufacturing too, with all kinds of new-fangled garden tools on sale, and, eventually, the first lawn mower. The search was on for bigger, brighter and better plants. Countries, such as those in South America, were being opened up for exploration, and many plants came from there to grace conservatories, Wardian cases (see page 44) or flower borders. Those who had no gardens were able to enjoy colourful flowers in the municipal parks, where carpet bedding, complete with floral clocks and coats of arms, became an art form.

Order returned to the garden; the idealized landscapes of 'Capability' Brown and the 18th century were swept aside. The typical Victorian villa had delusions of grandeur and became a country house in miniature. The idea was to ape the layouts of the great estates. Carpet bedding was used to imitate the parterres of a century or so earlier: fuchsias, geraniums, lobelias, dahlias – all the flowers we use today – were set out in patterns and rows, usually in garish colour groupings. Ideas for these layouts were published regularly in magazines such as *The Gardener's Chronicle*, but were nothing more than simplified versions of the Elizabethan knot. Villa owners also bought monkey puzzle trees, which they had seen in the gardens of large estates such as ERDDIG (Clwyd), little realizing that they would block out the light in already gloomily furnished rooms, and wreck newly-laid paving with their invasive roots.

The romantic wilderness of the 18th century, a grove of shrubs and trees, was copied widely in gardens of countless suburban villas, where it became the shrubbery – a dismal collection of evergreens, spotted laurel, privet and box, or sometimes rhododendrons with their leathery leaves coated with grime from the grim industrial smoke that hung over most towns and cities.

The garden came indoors, too, and both flower arranging and drying flowers for winter became popular hobbies. There were elaborate table decorations concentrating on ferns. These were very much in fashion, and unscrupulous fern vendors dug them up in the wild and sold them in the towns where pollution would almost certainly kill the plants off. Some ferns were luckier, however, and were kept in specially-built fern houses or ferneries, often with rockeries in the background. There is a fine indoor fern house designed by James Wyatt at Tatton Park in Cheshire, and a good restored fernery at Kingston Lacy in Dorset.

All sorts of plants were collected. Jane Loudon gave instructions in her magazine on building a moss house which had rustic pillars and laths on which mosses of all different kinds were displayed. 'Moss work' had become popular and she

MONKEY PUZZLE TREE

Left *A Byzantine urn in the sunk garden at Nymans*

suggested 'arranging the moss in an arabesque pattern, with different colours combined something like those of a Turkey carpet . . . or with . . . the crest of the family'. The Wardian case (invented originally to transport plants safely home from abroad during long sea voyages) grew to the size of a large floral cabinet and was filled with lilies and aspidistras, and tulips too, for bulbs had now come down in price. Scented-leaved geraniums were fashionable, newly imported from South Africa, and pots of them were set on the stairs so that the ladies' gowns brushed against them as they passed, releasing their perfume.

When the tax on glass was repealed in 1845, there was a rush to build conservatories; considered suitable for ladies to garden in, most were heated in some way. Camellias (still thought to be tender), jasmine and stephanotis were favourite plants for the conservatory, together with geraniums and fuchsias. Subtropical plants such as ferns, palms and orchids were also popular, and in fact the 20th edition of *Abercrombie's Every Man His Own Gardener*, published in 1813, encouraged its readers to 'cultivate collections of the most curious and singular exotic plants from the various different and most distant hot parts of the known world'. The inevitable insects were dealt with by spraying them with a mixture of soap and water, or nicotine. And if all else failed, there was always Keating's Persian Insect-Destroying Powder which might well have destroyed the gardener too; all sorts of toxic remedies, such as mercury, were used as insecticides.

Rock gardens such as the one at ALTON TOWERS (Staffordshire) were all the rage, with Lady Broughton's at Hoole in Cheshire representing 'the mountains of Savoy'. Matterhorns in miniature came into vogue, the worst ones built with piles of clinker from conservatory boilers, with tin chamonix goats perched on them. A writer of the day said sternly: 'Rock work, whenever it is intended to be formed, should always be constructed with one kind of stone; not, as usually seen, made up of petrifactions of building bricks from kilns . . . altogether a rubbish-like assemblage.'

Roses were an important component of the Victorian garden and all the big estates had a rosery – DYFFRYN BOTANIC GARDEN (South Glamorgan) is one example. Villa owners preferred to keep their roses neatly arranged as standards, planting one in the centre of each ornamental bed.

Every self-respecting Victorian garden had to have a lawn, now that the mower, invented in 1830, made maintenance simpler. After the early days, when it needed two men to push it, the mower had become relatively lightweight and easy to use – there was even a version for ladies for six shillings. (Lawn mowers were often pulled by ponies with special shoes before the arrival of the motor-powered mower.)

With the use of cast iron, garden furniture became highly decorative – if uncomfortable to sit on. A short-lived rustic movement, when garden furniture and trellis were made from hewn branches of trees, influenced cast-iron furniture

OTHER VICTORIAN GARDENS
Peckover House at Wisbech (Cambridgeshire) has good examples of trees the Victorians loved to plant, including the monkey puzzle and the ginkgo. Harewood House (West Yorkshire) boasts a magnificent terrace designed in 1840 by Sir Charles Barry, a fashionable architect of the day. Other 19th-century gardens worth seeing are at Abbotsford, near Melrose (Borders), and Inigo Thomas's design at Athelhampton (Dorset). For curiosity value, see Lord Redesdale's Japanese garden at Batsford, Moreton-in-Marsh (Gloucestershire), created in the 1890s.

too, which was often moulded in imitation. The temples of the 18th century gave way to summerhouses, often decorative, which were usually made from wood.

At their worst, the Victorians were ostentatious and vulgar; at their best, sumptuous and colourful. But, like them or laugh at them, their influence remains. It is seen not only in our public parks, but also (and most notably) in hanging baskets, boxes and tubs, where a jingoistic combination of red, white and blue – geraniums, lobelia and aubretia – is still the most popular choice.

◆

GARDENING UNDER GLASS

Flat glass was not invented until about the 1st century AD and so the earliest greenhouses, made by the Romans, used mica instead. They were used to 'force' vegetables such as cucumbers, and for roses and lilies. The idea of growing plants under glass was revived in the 17th century when the craze for exotic and unusual plants, including tender citrus fruits, demanded the erection of some form of shelter during the winter in northern Europe. Oranges and lemons were displayed on the terrace in tubs in the summer, but in winter they needed cover. Henrietta Maria, wife of Charles I, built an enclosed 'oringe garden' to protect her trees, but it would have had very little glass in it. From the idea of rooms like these, the first orangeries were developed. Soon they became permanent decorative buildings with relatively large glazed windows, though the roofs remained solid.

No one had yet realized the importance of light and circulation of air, as well as heat, in keeping plants healthy. Sir Thomas Hanmer, a friend of John Evelyn, wrote in his *Garden Book* about a 'winter-house' which must be used with judgement lest it kills more plants than are preserved. The place, he said, should be lofty with large windows and doors on the south side alone, to be opened on mild days to let in the 'gentle' air, but tightly shut against frosts. On 'violent cold nights' the place might be warmed with a pan of coals or a stove.

The largest and most impressive orangery was built for Louis XIV at Versailles in 1685. It was 508 ft (155 m) long, 42 ft (13 m) wide and 45 ft (14 m) high, and housed more than a thousand orange trees. The first orangeries were heated by braziers, then by stoves placed inside them, which probably gave off noxious fumes and may have damaged the plants. Ahead of his time, John Evelyn produced a design for a heated greenhouse, in 1691, with a furnace outside the building and a suction system taking out the 'tainted effete and imprisoned old air' and replacing it with 'a fresh supply from without'. John Evelyn is credited with the first use of the word 'greenhouse' (that is, a place to grow tender 'evergreens'), and he also used the word 'conservatory' for the first time in 1664.

The magnificent domed conservatory at Syon Park

One of the earliest greenhouses remaining was built at CHATSWORTH (Derbyshire) in 1698, about ten years later than Wren's greenhouse for King William of Orange and Queen Mary at HAMPTON COURT PALACE (London). At that time these buildings had a solid back wall and roof and windows along the front, and were used to grow pomegranates and myrtles, as well as citrus plants. There is a ravishing greenhouse of this period, built *c.* 1685, on the third terrace at POWIS CASTLE (Powys).

With the development of cast iron from the 1760s onwards, and the possibilities that went with it for lighter, stronger structures, it became feasible (thanks to the invention of curved iron glazing bars in 1816, patented by J.C. Loudon) to make larger and larger freestanding glasshouses with glass roofs to go with them, letting in more light. One of the first of these was Nash's conservatory at Barnsley Park in Gloucestershire, and one of the most impressive was Charles Fowler's domed conservatory at SYON PARK (London).

At CHATSWORTH (Derbyshire), the 6th Duke of Devonshire and his head gardener, Joseph Paxton, decided to build what was to be the largest greenhouse in the world: the Great Conservatory or 'Great Stove'. It took four years to build (1836–40), and was 227 ft (69 m) long, 123 ft (38 m) wide and 67 ft (20 m) high, covering three-quarters of an acre (0.3 ha). Coal to heat it had to be brought in huge quantities along a hidden underground tunnel. In it Paxton cultivated the huge water-lily *Victoria amazonica* – its 7 ft (2 m) wide leaves supported the weight of his small daughter. Sadly, the building no longer exists, for it was far too expensive to heat, and the 9th Duke blew it up just after World War I. You can still see the outline of its walls in the grounds. Another of Paxton's designs for CHATSWORTH, however, has survived intact: the Conservative Wall, a series of stepped conservatories finished in 1848.

Paxton went on to design something even more ambitious – the Crystal Palace. This huge structure, built in Hyde Park for the Great Exhibition of 1851, was 2100 ft (640 m) long, 400 ft (122 m) wide and covered 19 acres (7.6 ha). It was later dismantled and re-erected in south London, where it remained until it was destroyed by fire not long before World War II.

From 1826 onwards piped hot-water systems became readily available, and in the late 1830s the first sheet glass was produced, bringing with it the possibility of having really large panes in windows. Soon after, in 1845, the iniquitous tax on glass was repealed, leaving the way clear for experiment.

Now the owners of large estates vied with each other to build larger and better glasshouses. The Royal Botanic Gardens at KEW (London) built the Palm House (now restored) in 1848, while ordinary gardeners built conservatories on to their houses or contented themselves with bell-shaped cloches or garden frames which were stood over hot-beds (manure-filled pits which generated their own natural heat). Plants were also grown in Wardian cases. Nathanial Bagshaw Ward,

BICTON PARK'S PALM HOUSE

WARDIAN CASE

44

a London doctor, discovered that plants would thrive in sealed glass containers provided they had light and moisture. He put it to the practical use of transporting plants, but the idea caught on, and 'Wardian cases' were soon to be seen in prosperous homes, some of them built like the Crystal Palace in miniature, and some set into window frames.

Many people at that time constructed what were called winter gardens, which were heated conservatories on a large scale with fewer plants and more seating and walking space. Here palms and other exotic plants were grown. It became fashionable to entertain in them, and many of the newly-created seaside resorts built winter gardens where orchestras played and people strolled, protected from the inclement weather.

Greenhouses themselves have become less decorative since the 19th century, but now come in a variety of new shapes and sizes. Indeed, there seems to be a swing in fashion away from the freestanding greenhouse at the end of the garden towards the more decorative conservatory – often 'Victorian' in design. Heating a freestanding greenhouse can be expensive, as the Victorians found out, so we tend to bring our exotic plants indoors. Living in centrally-heated houses, we are able to grow these attractive, but tender, 'greenhouse' plants as part of our interior decoration.

SOME WINTER GARDENS
Splendid winter gardens are to be found at Rhyl (Clwyd), which has been converted into a butterfly sanctuary, and at Avery Hill Park in Eltham (London), which has a 90 ft (27 m) dome, restored in the 1970s.

BUDDLEIA DAVIDII

PLANT HUNTERS AND PIONEERS

It is hard for us to remember, when we walk around the average back garden today, just how many of the plants growing there are not native to this country. Forsythia, with its yellow spring flowers, is a Chinese plant, while privet is from Japan; berberis comes from Chile and the flowering currant from North America. Over the centuries, explorers and plant hunters have risked their lives – and in some cases lost them – in the quest for new species, combing Europe, the Near and Far East, the Americas and Australasia. Names such as *Incarvillea delavayi*, *Buddleia davidii*, *Rhododendron souliei* and *Rosa fargesi* are plant names commemorating the men, many of them French, who first brought them to Europe: Jean-Marie Delavay, Jean Pierre Armand David, Jean André Soulié and Paul Guillaume Farges.

The first people to bring exotic plants to Europe were probably the Moors, who are known to have brought roses and jasmine to Spain from Persia. Then the Spaniards themselves, on their expeditions to the New World, brought back the passion flower, nasturtium and marigold. In the 16th century there was an influx of plants from Turkey, notably the tulip, hyacinth and anemone, and the crown imperial (*Fritillaria imperialis*). Although the latter originated in the

Scarlet rhododendrons in the gardens at Leonardslee

Himalayas, it is believed to have been introduced into Europe by the ambassador of the Holy Roman Empire, Ghiselin de Busbecq.

By the 17th century, when John Parkinson published his *Paradisus*, more plants had been brought to Europe, this time by the French. The *Robinia pseudo-acacia* was introduced at this time, as was the Canada lily (*Lilium canadense*), both from North America. The hollyhock, lilac and hardy hibiscus had also arrived from Turkey. The Tradescants, father and son, were active at this time, visiting North America, and two cottage garden plants – the golden rod and Michaelmas daisy – began to appear in British gardens, together with specimen trees such as the liquidambar and the stag's horn sumach. Many plant collectors were missionaries, or Jesuit priests travelling on church business. They were able to enter countries like China which were forbidden to other foreigners. Others, like Joseph Hooker, were doing a geological or geographical survey.

Collectors were not always received graciously by the countries they visited. Sir Joseph Banks wrote of the hostile reception he and Captain Cook received when they landed at Rio de Janeiro in Brazil: 'Instead of being received as friends and allies of His Most Faithful Majesty, orders were immediately issued out that every insult possible should be offered to the officers of our ship.' Others were financed by wealthy patrons, or even a syndicate of people. Employees of the East India Company also brought in plants, notably in the early 1800s.

The first plants brought back by sailing ship had little chance of survival – probably about one in a thousand. All kinds of weird containers were used: for example, the roots were enclosed in the bladders of animals, in hard clay, or in wooden boxes. Some sea-captains were better than others at this task, and there is a variety of camellia named after Captain Rawes of the ship *Warren Hastings*, who brought the plant back safely from China. Captain Bligh, charged with a cargo of bread-fruit trees, made the crew give up their water rations to keep the plants alive. Then in 1829 Dr Nathanial Ward thought of a way of transporting them in sealed glass carrying cases (see page 45) and indirectly started the tea-growing industry in India, when 20,000 tiny tea plants were sent from Shanghai in China to the Himalayas.

The end of the 19th and beginning of the 20th centuries, with improved communications and better transportation, saw the heyday of plant collecting. DYFFRYN BOTANIC GARDEN (South Glamorgan) was designed at the turn of the century to house the plants collected by Sir John Cory and his son Reginald, and the botanist George Maw filled his garden at BENTHALL HALL (Shropshire) with plants from the Mediterranean.

In 1898 a young man of 23, Ernest Wilson, was sent to China to find the handkerchief tree (*Davidia involucrata*). Travellers had brought back pressed leaves with their strange white bracts but no seed. Wilson was away for three years and found not only the handkerchief tree but hundreds of other plants,

FRITILLARIA IMPERIALIS

notably the *Magnolia delavayi*. More expeditions followed, and on one he saw a superb, hitherto unknown, lily across a narrow gorge. While trying to reach it he smashed his leg and almost had to have it amputated on the spot. But he brought the precious plant – *Lilium regale* – safely back home.

Perhaps the greatest character among the plant hunters was Reginald Farrer, the alpine expert and author of many standard works on rock gardens. He was a purist who despised the rockeries of his day, calling them 'almond puddings' and 'dogs' graves'. He was also hard on the edelweiss, describing it as 'the Flannel flower of the Alps'. In 1914 Farrer went on a plant-collecting expedition to the border of Tibet, bringing back the guelder rose (*Viburnum fragrans*). He nearly came to grief on this expedition when his horse, Spotted Fat ('one-eyed, sullen and demoniacal'), slipped on a ramshackle wooden bridge and they fell into a ravine (remarkably, they both survived). Farrer became a Buddhist as a result of his expeditions to China and Tibet.

An eccentric stocky figure wearing shorts and an old pith helmet, with his socks round his ankles, Farrer's last expedition was to a remote Burmese valley. In his last letter home he wrote that his mountain hut was full of paper trays of seeds which he was trying to dry in a warm, wet, sunless climate. He was finally defeated by a combination of exhaustion and driving rain. The seeds never reached England and Farrer died, probably from pneumonia, on 17 October 1920 at the age of 40.

THE HERBACEOUS BORDER

Although the herbaceous border is generally believed to be the brainchild of William Robinson and Gertrude Jekyll at the end of the 19th and beginning of the 20th centuries, the idea of massing hardy plants together in one large bed goes back probably to Tudor times, and certainly existed in the 1730s at Philip Southcote's gentleman's country residence at Woburn Farm in Surrey. His continuous flower border consisted of hollyhocks, golden rods and crown imperials, planted in order of height, with an edging of pinks at the front, and roses, sweet briar, lilac and syringa behind. In the mid 1800s, swimming against the tide of fashion, the Warburton family, at Arley Hall in Cheshire, planted double borders of flowering perennials which still exist today. Despite the formal look of Victorian gardens, most of the large houses still grew old-fashioned flowering plants, but these were usually grown in rows in the kitchen gardens, to be cut for the house.

What Robinson and Jekyll did was capture and popularize the late-Victorian reaction to regimented planting and a nostalgia for old-fashioned flowers instead

The white garden at Hidcote Manor, created by Lawrence Johnston

of the gaudy colours of geraniums and other traditional bedding plants. Although the tradition of carpet bedding died hard, it was not long before the herbaceous border became all the rage, backed enthusiastically by people like William Morris and the Arts and Crafts movement. Bare earth was out and beds were crammed with plants. The 'new' herbaceous border had a great deal to commend it, for it was less labour-intensive than using half-hardy plants, which had to be dug up at the end of each season and discarded or overwintered in a greenhouse or conservatory – a costly and time-consuming process. Apart from staking, and perhaps cutting down at the end of the season, the herbaceous plants would more or less look after themselves, and only need dividing and replanting every four years or so.

William Robinson was a bluff, aggressive self-made man, coming from a humble background in Ireland, a working gardener turned writer and publisher. Gertrude Jekyll belonged to a rich, cultured family, had trained as a painter, and had no need to earn a living. Failing eyesight in her fifties forced her to give up painting and switch to gardening. She contributed to, then briefly edited, Robinson's magazine *The Garden*, and an enduring friendship was forged.

As writers, they spread their gospel effectively through books and magazines, advocating the use of half-forgotten old-fashioned cottage plants and taking advantage of the new hardy perennials that were coming in from abroad. Their views, however, were not totally in accord. Robinson was a purist, firmly believing that only hardy plants should be used and that they should be grouped together as they are found in the wild – a concept he put to work in his garden at Gravetye Manor in Sussex. No 'specimen plants from the greenhouse' were allowed under any circumstances.

Gertrude Jekyll, on the other hand, preferred a less rigid scheme, using annuals and, on occasions, half-hardy plants as well. As a painter she had learnt about colour and its relation to light and thus handled colour brilliantly in the garden, planning borders that changed gradually along their length from pastel shades to vivid tones and back again. She was also the first person to advocate the one-colour border, and her first single-tone garden at Munstead Wood in Surrey, the house built for her by Sir Edwin Lutyens, was a grey one. 'Grey helps all the colours gain in purity and brilliance,' she said, and wrote at the time: 'I badly want others, and especially a gold garden, a blue garden and a green garden.' Her definitive work on the subject, *Colour in the Flower Garden*, was published in 1908, when she wrote of pastel borders: 'White flowers are the only ones that possess the advantage of heightening the tone of flowers which have only a light tint of colour,' and 'any experienced colourist knows that the blues will be more telling – more purely blue – by the juxtaposition of a rightly placed complementary colour.' Almost all her one-colour borders were heightened in this way – she often used just one or two plants in sharp yellow, for instance, to point up a

HOLLYHOCK

border in blue. These ideas were to be taken up later, with brilliant effect, by Lawrence Johnston at HIDCOTE MANOR (Gloucestershire) and then Vita Sackville-West with her white garden at SISSINGHURST CASTLE (Kent).

A true herbaceous border flowers only for a short time in the summer and needs plenty of space so that one can stand well back and admire it. It also has to be allowed to lie fallow in the winter time, so is only really suitable for very large gardens. The garden writer Christopher Lloyd still maintains his father's enormous herbaceous border at GREAT DIXTER (East Sussex). Over 200 ft (60 m) long, it is a classic example of the herbaceous border.

The new 'mixed' border, on the other hand, with shrubs, even trees in the background, and annuals and bedding plants used to fill in the gaps, can be kept going for much of the year and is better suited to a smaller space. It was used to brilliant effect in the 1930s by garden designers such as Percy Cane at Dartington Hall in Devon, and later by Lanning Roper, the American landscape designer whose work can be seen at WISLEY (Surrey). Today the mixed border will be found in the garden of almost any self-respecting country house, and even in town gardens, but there are still outstanding examples such as Peter Healing's borders at THE PRIORY (Hereford and Worcester) or those at KNIGHTSHAYES COURT (Devon).

OTHER HERBACEOUS BORDERS
Lytes Cary (Somerset) has a colourful long border backed by roses and attractive climbers, while at Leeds Castle (Kent) there are some unusually-planted triangular beds of herbaceous plants, designed by Russell Page but recently developed further.

THE LAWN

Britain is famous throughout the world for its lush green lawns. Like Ireland, we have our temperate, humid climate to thank for this. Almost anywhere else in the world lawns are maintained only with considerable effort. The hotter, drier summers and colder winters of the Continent or continental America, for example, make lawns difficult to establish and keep up; only in coastal areas do lawns flourish. This may well explain the few references to grass in descriptions of the gardens of ancient Persia, Greece and Rome.

In this country the first lawns, it seems, were laid within the walls of castles, where a courtyard or inner area would be turfed so that the inhabitants could escape the smells, and probably the rats and mice, that lurked indoors in summer. The grass was kept down by trampling on it, beating it, or allowing sheep to graze on it. The gardens of monasteries often had an area of grass, too, probably alongside the herber, or herb garden, where the monks could walk in meditation.

We have to go to medieval times to find real evidence of what early lawns were like. When the great plague swept across Europe from 1348, townspeople rushed to the countryside in an attempt to avoid it. In a description of the country, Boccaccio in the *Decameron* records: 'A meadow plot of green grass, powdered with a thousand flowers.' These 'flowery meads' were, according to contemporary paintings, likely to include daisies, primroses, pinks, periwinkles and speedwell, and taller flowers such as white camomile and marguerites. Lawns were often made entirely of camomile at this time.

One of the first-ever gardening books, *The Advantages of Country Living*, written by the Italian Pietro de Crescenzi, who died in 1305, explains how to lay a lawn, advising the reader first to dig out all weeds and roots and scald the soil to sterilize it. The turfs were treated more roughly than they are today – Pietro tells us to tramp the grass down so that it cannot be seen, 'when fresh growth will appear'. There is another account, 200 years later, where the author goes even further, saying that the turfs should be laid grass-side downwards 'and afterward daunced upon with the feete . . . within a short time after, the grass may begin to peepe up and put foorth like small haires'.

In medieval times the lawn itself – cut twice a year by scythes – was often surrounded by turfed benches, constructed on mounds of soil. There is a record of 1300 turfs being delivered to Windsor Castle in 1311 for this purpose. These seats must have often become sodden and uncomfortable to sit on after a shower of rain. But no doubt the thick layers of clothing worn at that time, particularly by the ladies, kept the damp out.

In Tudor times lawns were turned into playgrounds. Henry VIII, who did not care much for flowers, insisted that the grass at HAMPTON COURT PALACE (London) was made over to sporting pleasures. Apart from archery, bowls was the most popular sport, though one can imagine the difficulty of keeping the turf close-cut at all times by 'mowing and rowling'. Long-handled scythes were used, and servant women followed behind the scyther, sweeping the grass and gathering up the cuttings into primitive wheelbarrows. About this time camomile lawns came into fashion, possibly because they were slower growing. It is now thought by some that the green on which Drake played his famous bowls match was actually camomile, and not grass.

In the 17th century lawns continued to become more and more popular, especially among the large landowners. A French gardening expert wrote, enviously, that in England the lawns were so exquisite that 'in France we can scarce ever hope to come up to it'.

The 18th century ushered in the age of the grand landscape garden. William Kent, 'Capability' Brown and their disciples decreed that there should be great sweeps of grass among the plantings of trees, the lakes, and the classical features of great houses such as BLENHEIM PALACE (Oxfordshire). The grass would be close-cut near the house, evolving into meadow land beyond. New tools such as shears and edging irons were employed to keep the grass immaculate, and horse-drawn rollers were used, the horses wearing woollen 'socks' or leather pads over their hooves so they would not damage the turf. These large areas of lawn were

Right *A statue on the lawns in the water parterre at Studley Royal*

incredibly labour-intensive: the close-cropped lawns had to be scythed twice a month, and Hugh Walpole mentions employing 50 weeding women to keep the grass looking pristine.

The industrial revolution, together with the rapid growth of large towns and the construction of suburban villas in the 19th century, brought lawns to the bourgeoisie and merchant classes. Fortunately, in 1830 Edwin Budding, a worker in a textile factory in Stroud, invented the lawn mower. He adapted a machine for trimming the nap of cloth, a cylinder of blades set in a spiral, for garden use. Within a couple of years the first Ransome mower was on sale for seven guineas, with a larger model 'preferable for workmen' available. A family snapshot taken in the 1860s shows a lady, complete with hat and bustle, mowing the grass while her husband sits and watches! Then the horse-drawn mower made its appearance, followed by petrol-driven versions which were used in most stately homes at the turn of the century. Another breakthrough came in the 1960s when the first lightweight electric mowers came on to the market.

18TH-CENTURY HORSE LAWN BOOTS

The lawn lapsed for a while in World War II, when citizens were urged to dig up the grass and grow vegetables instead. Today, the lawn is more popular than ever, cut, not twice a year as in medieval times, but up to twice a week in summer. Purpose-made mixes of grass are available for shady conditions, for hard wear, or for that bowling-green finish. The lawn today is fed and weeded with the aid of chemicals, and mown swiftly, scarified and trimmed with electrically-powered machines. However, in spite of all the gadgets, that coveted green stripe so loved by head gardeners remains best achieved by the direct descendant of Edwin Budding's machine, the cylinder mower.

FAMOUS FLOWERS IN HISTORY

Botanists and plant breeders never give up their search for that elusive perfect flower. There is a fortune waiting for anyone who can produce a blue rose, a pink daffodil or a truly black tulip; we are never, it seems, satisfied with what we already have. Many of the most beautiful flowers have a prosaic history behind them – the Madonna lily, for instance, whose bulbs were eaten by the Romans as a delicacy and pounded into an ointment to ease corns. Violets were used as a sweetener in food in the Middle Ages before sugar was introduced to this country, and the saffron crocus is still grown today for culinary purposes rather than as a decorative flower. Our popular flowers come from all over the world. Sometimes a flower's name belies its origin: the French marigold actually comes from Mexico, while Old English lavender is a Mediterranean plant, brought here by the Romans.

The first dahlias were found by Spanish explorers in Mexico, growing like vines among trees. They were eventually brought into Europe but nobody knew what to do with them – the French tried to cook the tubers like potatoes, and in England they were used for animal food. In Victorian times they finally became fashionable as flowers, with high prices (as much as 200 guineas) being asked for a plant. The dahlia's popularity peaked again just after World War II. Current fashion dictates that the smaller compact varieties are more chic than the large mop-headed ones.

There are many stories to be told about how varieties and colours of flowers have evolved over the centuries, but the most romantic story of all must be that of the rose. Roses were known in ancient China, but during the rule of Nero they became a passionate cult in the Roman empire, so much so that olive groves and orchards were grubbed up and turned over to their cultivation. They also grew roses in the first heated greenhouses and, to keep up with the insatiable demand, imported them from Egypt and Greece (Rhodes is named after the red roses grown there for the Romans).

TULIP

Roses were used instead of laurel wreaths, and to carpet banqueting rooms. At one party, guests were pelted with roses and some suffocated under the petals. They were also used for garlands and cooked in food. Their petals, which were believed to be an aphrodisiac, were floated on the surface of wine.

Although much loved in medieval and Tudor times, the rose fell out of fashion in Britain during the centuries that followed, but not in France. Napoleon's Empress, Josephine, was responsible for the first great rose garden at her house at Malmaison on the outskirts of Paris. Her gardeners combed the world to bring back more and more varieties to stock it. She then commissioned a painter, Pierre-Joseph Redouté, to make records of her collection of flowers. The first hybrid tea roses (now called large-flowered roses), the most popular varieties today, were bred in the 1860s. The most famous of these is 'Peace', raised by the Meilland nursery at Lyons just before the outbreak of World War II and originally given the name of Mme Antoine Meilland. War came, and just before France fell, Monsieur Meilland put several plants on one of the last planes to leave the country for the USA. There they were raised by an American nursery, and at the Peace Conference at the end of the war, a bunch of the roses was put at each place – and 'Peace' got its name.

AURICULA

The tulip is another flower with a fascinating history. Originally brought to Europe from Turkey in the 1500s, they did not attract much attention at first. But they got into the hands of Flemish botanist Carolus Clusius, who began to ask such high prices for his bulbs that everyone wanted them, and tulipmania began. It was not the growers but speculators who pushed the prices up. Tulip Notes for the bulbs were traded like 'Futures' on the Dutch stock exchange, and fortunes were often won and lost without anyone actually seeing the bulbs

The rose, seen here at Wisley in plenty, has a long romantic history – it was particularly fashionable in Roman times

themselves, prices reaching as much as £1500 for a single bulb. Eventually the Dutch Government stepped in and stopped the trade, and it was a long time before they became the cheap bulbs they are today. But tulipmania has not quite subsided. The search for the black tulip goes on, and in 1960 bulbs for a green-flowered variety were sold at over £200 per lb.

Over the centuries many other flowers have become the objects of high fashion. The Huguenot weavers brought over the little auricula with them at the end of the 16th century, when they fled to England. Auriculas became all the rage and people would pay a week's wages just to own one, and travel miles to view a new variety. Auriculas, with their curiously artificial-looking 'painted' faces, were displayed on mock theatre stages, with cardboard scenery around them. All kinds of secret remedies were used to produce the perfect show plant – it was believed by some growers that raw meat, dug into the soil around them, was beneficial.

In Scotland – in Paisley in particular – there was a passion for growing pinks, while in the north of England, around Cheshire and Lancashire, the polyanthus was popular. From these passions the first flower shows developed. Bodies like the Royal Horticultural Society, formed in 1804, began to hold fêtes which became larger and more important as the years went on, culminating in the first Chelsea Flower Show in 1912.

◆

THE SOUTH-WEST AND WALES

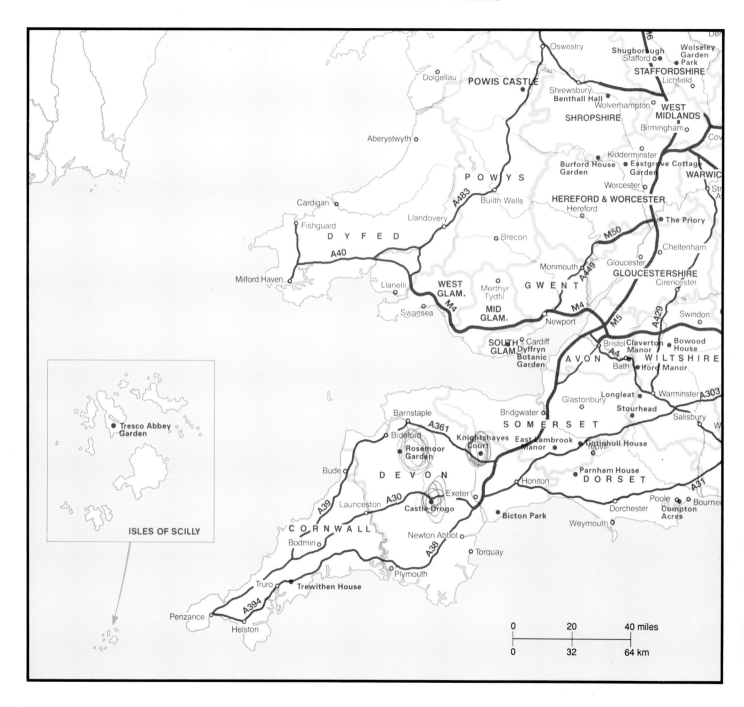

Map labels:

Oswestry

Shugborough
Stafford
Wolseley Garden Park
STAFFORDSHIRE
Lichfield

Dolgellau

POWIS CASTLE

Shrewsbury
Benthall Hall
Wolverhampton
WEST MIDLANDS
SHROPSHIRE
Birmingham
Cov

Aberystwyth

Kidderminster
Burford House Garden
Eastgrove Cottage Garden
WARWIC

POWYS

Worcester
HEREFORD & WORCESTER
Hereford

Cardigan

A483
Builth Wells

Str
A

Fishguard

Llandovery

The Priory

DYFED

Brecon

M50
Cheltenham

A40

Monmouth
Gloucester
GLOUCESTERSHIRE
Cirencester

Milford Haven

Llanelli

WEST GLAM.
Merthyr Tydfil
GWENT
A449

Swindon

Swansea
MID GLAM.

M4
Newport
M4
M5
A429

SOUTH GLAM.
Cardiff
Dyffryn Botanic Garden

Bristol
Claverton Manor
Bowood House
WILTSHIRE

AVON
A4
Bath
Iford Manor

Barnstaple

Bridgwater

SOMERSET
Longleat
Stourhead
Warminster
A303

Glastonbury
Salisbury

A361

Bideford

Knightshayes Court
East Lambrook Manor
Tintinhull House

Rosemoor Garden

Bude

DEVON

Parnham House
DORSET

A39
Launceston
A30
Castle Drogo
Exeter
Honiton

Poole
A31
Bourne
Compton Acres
Dorchester

Bodmin

Newton Abbot
A38
Bicton Park

Weymouth

CORNWALL

Torquay

Plymouth

Truro
Trewithen House

A394
Penzance
Helston

0   20   40 miles
0   32   64 km

Isles of Scilly inset

Tresco Abbey Garden

ISLES OF SCILLY

58

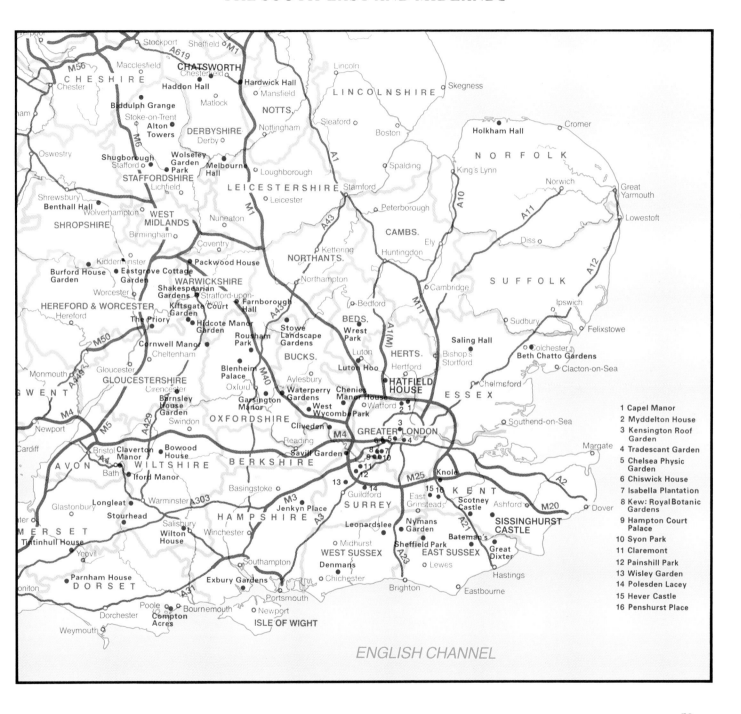

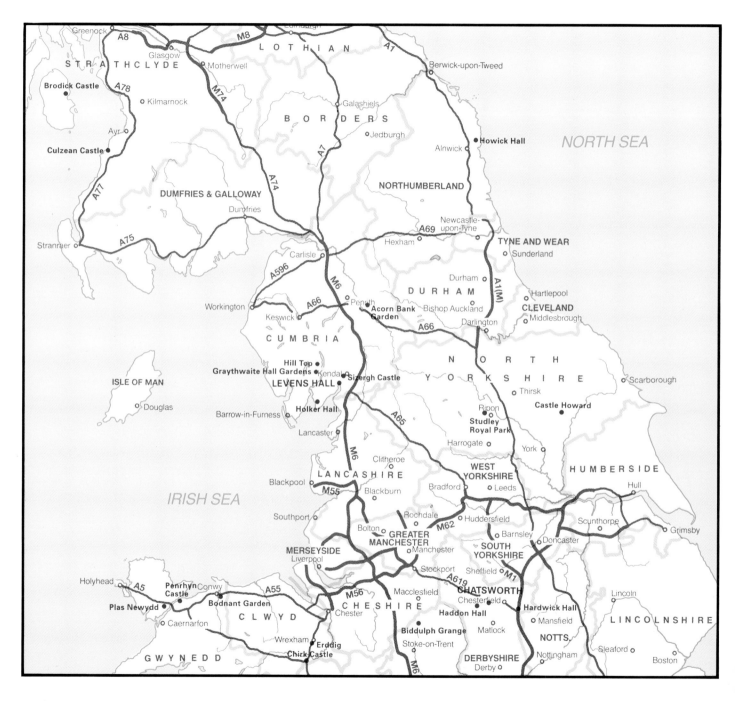

SCOTLAND

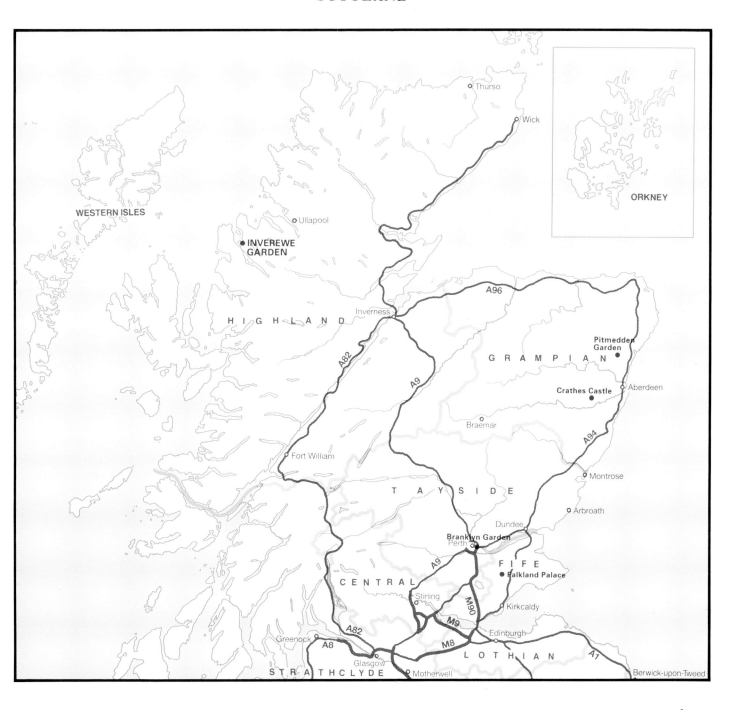

WESTERN ISLES

ORKNEY

○ Thurso

○ Wick

○ Ullapool

● INVEREWE
GARDEN

H I G H L A N D

Inverness ○

A96

G R A M P I A N

● Pitmedden
Garden

A82

A9

Crathes Castle ● ○ Aberdeen

○ Braemar

A94

○ Fort William

T A Y S I D E

○ Montrose

○ Arbroath

Dundee ○

Branklyn Garden
Perth ○

A9

F I F E

● Falkland Palace

C E N T R A L

Stirling ○

M90

○ Kirkcaldy

M9

A82

Edinburgh ○

Greenock ○

A8

M8

L O T H I A N

A1

S T R A T H C L Y D E

Glasgow ○

○ Motherwell

Berwick-upon-Tweed

2
Gazetteer

ACORN BANK GARDEN CUMBRIA

It looked at one stage as though this beautiful old 2½-acre (1 ha) garden would have to be closed for lack of funds, but a public appeal has ensured that it will remain open, at least for the time being. The tranquil garden, which is set on one side of the house, is divided in two. The larger part contains flower borders and an orchard, surrounded by splendid roses and a collection of clematis, including the unusual *C. chrysocoma*.

Acorn Bank is, however, best known for its physic garden with a collection of more than 250 different varieties of herbs. This is housed in what used to be the old walled vegetable garden, in which apricot, peach and nectarine trees still remain. A venerable quince tree forms a central point. All kinds of herbs are there, including witches' plants like belladonna and henbane.

The old greenhouse has many interesting plants including a datura with its curious trumpet-like flowers. In the orchard roses and fruits mix happily together, and in spring the grass underfoot is covered in bulbs: daffodils, species tulips, double white anemones and, later, lilies. At the back of the house is a bird reserve and a wild garden planted in the 1930s by a previous owner, Dorothy Una Ratcliffe.

The acorn bank, after which the house is named, goes down to a stream, Crowdundle Beck, and the Pennines can be glimpsed in the distance. Originally a religious retreat, adopted in the 13th century by the Knights Templars

Left Colourful herbaceous borders at Acorn Bank Garden

as a hospice, the red sandstone house is now used by the Sue Ryder Foundation.

Just north of Temple Sowerby, 6 miles
(9.5 km) east of Penrith, on the A66
(map page 60)

ALTON TOWERS STAFFORDSHIRE

Hiding behind the brash façade of one of Britain's brightest and best amusement parks – known as the Playground of the Potteries – are some magnificent grounds. More than 300 acres (120 ha) lie in the steep-sided valley of the River Churnet. Alton Towers itself, a huge 19th-century house now nothing more than a shell, was built by the architect A.W.N. Pugin. Once the home of the Earls of Shrewsbury, the estate came into its heyday in the early 1800s when the 15th Earl developed the gardens.

The estate includes several bizarre follies: the Druid's Sideboard was ordered by the 15th Earl as a replica of Stonehenge; a corkscrew fountain resembles a twist of barley sugar and a three-storey tower looks like a lighthouse with a stained-glass lantern on the top; there is a Roman bridge and a flag tower, and a Chinese pagoda which still spurts an enormous jet of water high into the air. The 16th Earl, nephew to the 15th, was responsible for most of the tree planting, including the tall graceful conifers.

The best way to visit the gardens in the first instance is to take the cable car, which gives you an aerial view of the grounds. You can then decide what to visit on foot.

An evening view of the pagoda fountain at Alton Towers

There is a large rockery with dwarf conifers as well as flowers, which is at its best in spring when the azaleas are in bloom. This is the place to see Victorian bedding at its grandest, packed with bright, gaudy plants. There are also Dutch and Italian gardens and, to add to the international look, a Swiss cottage perched high on the hillside.

$4\frac{1}{2}$ miles (7 km) east of Cheadle,
on the B5032 (map page 59)

BARNSLEY HOUSE GARDEN
GLOUCESTERSHIRE

Gardening writer Rosemary Verey owns this splendid garden, which surrounds a handsome 17th-century house. She cheerfully admits she knew little about gardening when she took it over, and learned as she went along.

Mrs Verey has used her knowledge of garden history to plan and plant many areas in historical styles. There is a formal knot garden made from box, with holly bushes shaved into topiary shapes. This is in sharp contrast to the 'wilderness', an area planted with young ornate trees. It is a very romantic garden, with a temple, a Gothick summer-house, and some wonderful vistas, notably the famous, much photographed laburnum walk, with alliums – decorative versions of the onion family – planted underneath. The trees are trained so that they meet overhead in an arch which rains lemon-yellow flowers in late May and early June.

One of Mrs Verey's latest additions is the *potager*, or French-style vegetable garden, which mixes flowers with vegetables and fruit, and shows you just how decorative simple things like massed lettuces can be, especially when contrasted with the strong foliage of chard and kale. There are plants for sale here, and the standard gooseberry trees can be ordered from Highfield Nurseries nearby.

4 miles (6.5 km) north-east of
Cirencester, off the A433 (map page 59)

BATEMAN'S   EAST SUSSEX

Situated in one of the Sussex Weald's most beautiful valleys, Bateman's is famous for being the much-loved home of author Rudyard Kipling from 1902 to 1936. It was here that he wrote many of his best-known books and poems. There is a happy domestic air about the 10 acres (4 ha) of gardens which lie to the south-west of the house and are really a series of outdoor rooms, edged by stone walls, borders of box or tall yew hedges. The Kiplings were responsible for laying out many of the paths and hedges, and also the rose garden and the pond, which was made specially so that it could be used for boating and bathing by the Kipling children.

The wide, flagged south terrace, which Kipling called 'The Quarter Deck', extends westwards to the boundary, and above the drawing-room window on the west front is a handsome *Campsis grandiflora*, whose tubular orange flowers appear in late summer. To the left of the front door is a rose, 'Maiden's Blush', a coloured relation of the white rose of York, which has been known since at least the 15th century. Look for the sundial on the edge of the formal garden; behind this is the original stone which marked Kipling's grave in Poet's Corner in Westminster Abbey.

Go through the gate to the west of the rose garden and the planting becomes less formal, with trees and flowering shrubs in rough grass carpeted with flowering bulbs in spring. The River Dudwell, which flows through the grounds, has banks flanked by the impressive foliage of the giant rhubarb-like gunnera, and the yellow arum-like skunk cabbage (*Lysichiton americanus*). Above them is a turkey oak, a silver weeping lime and a smoke tree (*Cotinus coggyria*). Look out, too, for the curiously-shaped nut tree (*Corylus avellana* 'Contorta'), which stands by the second footbridge leading over the stream to the mill, and, across the bridge, the sweet gum (*Liquidambar styraciflua*), whose leaves smell of varnish. A brick-laid, arched walk of fruit trees is under-planted with Solomon's Seal, bluebells, lilies-of-the-valley and other shade-loving plants. Look for domestic touches such as the bed of herbs by the brick wall, and the vegetable garden. There is an old watermill at the bottom of the gardens which still grinds corn for flour; alongside is one

Bateman's – the much-loved home of Rudyard Kipling

of the earliest working water-driven turbines in the world, installed by Kipling to generate electricity for the house.

**Half a mile (1 km) south-west of
Burwash, off the A265 (map page 59)**

BENTHALL HALL   SHROPSHIRE

In Victorian times this was the home of the botanist George Maw, who, having made a fortune out of tiles, devoted the rest of his life to scientific studies, and botany in particular. His first 20 years at Benthall were spent searching for new species of plants in mountainous regions of the Mediterranean, and then establishing them here in his own garden.

To display his prizes he built a rockery using boulders from a nearby quarry, and dug a type of cold frame (a ditch with a glass lid) to protect his alpines from the cold wet Shropshire winters. You can still see traces of it under a large laburnum tree. Some of his plants have, unfortunately, perished over the years, but the rockery is still full of unusual flowers. Maw's crocuses, planted a century ago, have now naturalized themselves in the long grass: in spring, *Crocus vernus* and *C. tommasinianus*, and in autumn, *C. pulchellus*, *C. speciosus* and the better-known *C. nudiflorus*.

There is also a pool garden with some pretty roses

around it, notably 'Felicia' (a hybrid musk) and the floribunda 'Gruss an Aachen' with creamy flowers. To one side of the house is a small topiary garden with toadstool-shaped bushes in yew and box, and a dovecote against whose walls you will see the peony *P. suffruticosa*.

**1 mile (1.5 km) north-west of Broseley,
on the B4375 (map pages 58–9)**

BETH CHATTO GARDENS   ESSEX

Beth Chatto's parents were both keen gardeners, but it was not until she met and married Andrew Chatto, a fruit grower, that her interest in plants – particularly plant ecology – was really kindled. The Chattos built their house at Elmstead Market in 1960. The site was not ideal: a dry, gravelly slope leading down to an area of water and clay where, Beth says, the cows 'sank up to their knees'.

Now the unusual and innovative gardens she has made there are known the world over, for their fine foliage plants in particular. The site has given her two gardens in one: a dry Mediterranean-style garden and a bog garden growing water-loving plants. The contrast between the fine silvery foliage of the one and the lush growth of the other is striking.

The original 4 acres (1.6 ha) were extended, and Beth Chatto started her now-famous nursery with the help of just one girl. Today it is a thriving business and, for people who do not have time to go round the gardens, she has planted island beds showing specimen plants for all sorts of situations. Beth Chatto believes that success in gardening is primarily a matter of choosing the right plant for the right place, not of seeing something pretty in a photograph and rushing off to buy it. And at White Barn House she gives us a living lesson, proving that having an excessively wet or dry soil can be turned to one's advantage.

**To the south-west of Elmstead Market,
on the A133 (map page 59)**

Part of Beth Chatto's beautiful gardens at White Barn House

BICTON PARK DEVON

Linked with the agricultural college which occupies the house nearby, this 60-acre (24 ha) estate came into being in its present form in the 18th century, when the formal Italian garden was built some way from the house on its south-eastern side. A series of imposing grassed terraces lead from a temple down to a pond with a fountain, with a vista on the far side of the valley which features an obelisk. There are some fine trees and shrubs including Irish yews beside the canal, with deodars at either end. On the terrace, encircling a stone seat, is a *Hiba arbor vita*, one of the famous 'Five Trees of Kiso' that was considered so valuable in 17th-century Japan that there was an order protecting it from being felled. Note too the Bull Bay magnolia lining the walls which can produce blooms 2 ft (60 cm) across. The splendid heated palm house, which was built in 1815–20, is one of the earliest glasshouses in the world to survive, and consists of hundreds of overlapping pieces of glass. Inside you will find a rain forest in miniature with Kentia palms 20 ft (6 m) high, bromeliads and tree ferns. Outside stands a sturdy Assam tea plant. Apart from the palm house there are many other greenhouses to visit, some containing half-hardy plants like geraniums and fuchsias, while the tropical house has colourful bougainvillea, hibiscus and strelitzias (bird of paradise flowers).

An oriental garden shows what an attractive alternative to paving raked gravel can be. Here you will find typical shrubs of China and Japan, including azaleas, camellias and maples, and a mulberry tree over 150 years old. The American garden boasts a snowdrop tree (*Halesia carolina*) and a calico bush with pink, waxy flowers. A curiosity of the hermitage garden by the lake is a summerhouse with walls lined with basketwork and the floor paved with knuckle-bones of deer. Nearby is a collection of dwarf conifers and over 2000 heathers. The amazing monkey puzzle avenue was laid out in 1842.

7 miles (11 km) north-east of Exmouth,
on the A376 (map page 58)

BIDDULPH GRANGE STAFFORDSHIRE

An example of the Victorian grand design at its most ornate, the gardens of Biddulph Grange were laid out in 15 acres (6 ha) of ground, on the edge of what was then moorland, in around 1842 by the rich industrialist James Bateman and his wife Maria. They later enlisted the help of the landscape designer and botanist Edward Cooke. No expense was spared, and what was basically a flat, rather boggy piece of land was transformed by moving tons of earth to create man-made hills and banks, while huge pieces of stone were brought in to form tunnels.

As is the case with many gardens of that time, it is not just one garden but several, starting off with a splendid balustraded terrace which fronts the house, complete with statuary and urns. This is flanked by a shrubbery, a large planting of rhododendrons, a bowling green, a quoits ground, and a 'stumpery'. There are also two fashionable gardens of the day: a 4-acre (1.6 ha) Chinese garden, enclosed by the Batemans' version of the Great Wall of China, complete with look-out tower, and containing also a decorative willow-pattern bridge, a pavilion, and a thicket of bamboos and maples; the Egyptian garden, guarded by sphinxes, has huge yew hedges that have been trained and clipped to look as though they might be the entrance to a tomb. The 'tomb' itself, made from local stone, houses nothing more than the statue of an ape, and becomes a cottage when you view it from the other side. This overlooks a pinetum which includes the Victorians' favourite tree, the monkey puzzle. The gardens have recently been saved and restored by a hard-working group of volunteers under the direction of the National Trust.

5 miles (8 km) south-east of Congleton,
off the A527 (map pages 59–60)

BLENHEIM PALACE OXFORDSHIRE

This is, quite simply, one of the most imposing parks and formal gardens in Britain, much of it laid out by 'Capability' Brown in the 1760s. As you enter through the

The formal garden to the east of Blenheim Palace

Triumphal Gate and see the sweep of the landscape, crowned by the vast palace, the lake, and Vanbrugh's Grand Bridge, it takes your breath away. The gardens at Blenheim have evolved gradually over a period of 200 years or more and provide a living monument of more than 2000 acres (800 ha) of British garden history.

The estate was originally presented to John Churchill, 1st Duke of Marlborough, by Queen Anne, to celebrate his victory at the Battle of Blenheim. Several famous designers had a hand in its development: first of all, Sir John Vanbrugh, who built a palace on the site in 1705 as a present from the grateful nation. At that time, Henry Wise, Queen Anne's gardener, started work on the grounds, probably under Vanbrugh's direction, creating gardens that were to match the house in grandeur. The first thing he created was a vast squared parterre. A 2-mile (3 km) avenue of elms was planted, stretching from the north-west front of the house. Many statues and fountains were added and, at the request of Sarah, Duchess of Marlborough, a flower garden.

The 4th Duke, however, had other ideas, and brought in the fashionable landscape gardener of his day, 'Capability' Brown. In an instant Henry Wise's formal parterres were ploughed up and replaced by parkland. But at the turn of the century there was a revival of interest in classical gardening, and the 9th Duke called in the French designer Achille Duchêne to restore some of Blenheim's formal splendour. Duchêne created the Italian garden, the scrolled parterre punctuated by topiary shapes to the east, and the lavish water parterre with black and gold fountains. Look carefully at the stonework on the terraces and you will spot a sphinx whose head is a likeness of Consuelo Vanderbilt, the American heiress who married the Duke. Another curiosity is one of the caryatids supporting the first terrace: the sculptor, Visseau, used Bert Timms, a young gardener on the estate, as his model. From the lower terrace, the drive winds up to the Temple of Diana, where Sir Winston Churchill proposed to Clementine.

The imposing bridge which now spans the vast, irregular lake was built by Vanbrugh over the then puny little River Glyme which meandered through the estate. He was mocked by the Duchess who thought the bridge vulgar and too ornate. 'Capability' Brown took one look at it and said it needed 'something worth crossing', so he dammed the river by creating a Great Cascade to the south of it, and formed the lake.

The 8-acre (3.2 ha) walled kitchen garden is one of the few pieces of Henry Wise's work to remain. Look for a domestic touch here – the bell in a niche in the northern wall which summoned a regiment of gardeners to work.

**9 miles (14.5 km) north-west of Oxford,
on the A34 (map page 59)**

BODNANT GARDEN   GWYNEDD

This 20th-century garden, carved out of inhospitable clay between 1904 and 1912 by the 2nd Lord Aberconway, is dominated by its great series of Italianate terraces, and the lush climate ensures that there is something to see all year round. Bodnant stretches over 80 acres (32 ha) of ground on the east side of the Conwy valley, looking across to Snowdonia. As well as the fine views of the river and mountains, it has the advantage of abundant running water and a backdrop of fine trees dating back to the 18th century. The garden is in two parts: the huge terraces, each with a different character and guarded by sphinxes around the house, and a lower, wild portion – known as 'the dell' – containing some splendid conifers.

Start your tour at the rose terrace, with its beds edged by saxifrages, helianthemums and dwarf campanulas. From here you have a stunning view down to the wooded valley of the River Conwy below, and across to the mountains of Snowdonia. Move on down to the croquet terrace below and admire the fountain edged with white wisteria, and the tall curved wall topped by a hedge of *Escallonia rubra macrantha* which provides shelter for a number of fine shrubs, such as the spring-flowering *Ceanothus rigidus*, the hydrangea-like *Viburnum macrocephalum* and a fine magnolia. Next comes the lily terrace, with a formal pond housing hybrid water-lilies in flower from June until late September, producing a thousand flowers or more. The lower rose terrace

The canal terrace at Bodnant Garden

follows, with some magnificent climbing roses scrambling over a pergola and more magnolias. Look, too, for outstanding plants like the green-flowered *Helleborus lividus corsicus* and *Euphorbia griffithii* 'Fireglow' with its bright bracts in summer. The canal terrace, next, houses more water-lilies and beds of herbaceous plants in grey-blue and purple. At the south end is Pin Mill, an attractive gazebo dating from 1730, once used as a mill and brought to Bodnant by the late Lord Aberconway. At the other end of the canal is the green theatre, a raised lawn-covered stage, with wings and backdrop of clipped yew.

Below, the formality turns into a profusion of camellias and magnolias, then a rock garden culminating in an apparently wild woodland dell, criss-crossed by paths and with a stream running through. The informality, however, has been carefully planned and planted with rhododendrons, camellias and azaleas, all growing under the shade of conifers; there is a wonderful selection of trees and shrubs, many of them brought to Britain by plant hunters of the time.

On your way out you will pass a tunnel of laburnums, transformed in early summer into arches of vivid yellow racemes.

8 miles (13 km) south of Llandudno
and Colwyn Bay, off the A470
(map page 60)

◆

BOWOOD HOUSE WILTSHIRE

When you go to Bowood, make straight for the lake, then stand back and look around you at one of the finest surviving landscapes by 'Capability' Brown. The 1st Earl of Shelburne commissioned Brown to lay out the estate in 1757 to complement the newly-built great house (now sadly demolished). All that remains today are the outbuildings which have been converted to make the present Shelburne family home, and the family mausoleum and orangery (now an art gallery) built by Robert Adam. Acting with his usual aplomb, and with 90 acres (36 ha) to play with, 'Capability' Brown dammed the waters of the Rivers Whetham and Washway below the house, to make an apparently natural 'lake' $1\frac{1}{2}$ miles (2.5 km) long. A Doric temple stands guard at the end of the lake path, and a hermit's cave lined with fossils and mineralogical specimens lies close to the head of the cascade.

The gardens have continued to evolve ever since. In the middle of the 18th century a walled garden was added, followed in the 19th century by the formal gardens to the south of the house, with their statues, topiary, urns and gravel walks, which are filled in summer with bright bedding flowers. In the 19th century, too, 60 acres (24 ha) of 'woodland' were planted, featuring rhododendrons and azaleas in great profusion. Other varieties of trees have been introduced since, and the arboretum now has more than 200 varieties of trees and shrubs.

Between Calne and Chippenham, off
the A4 (map pages 58–9)

◆

BRANKLYN GARDEN   TAYSIDE

This is a suburban garden that grew. Small, by the standards of other gardens in this book, it is, nevertheless, a fascinating place to visit, and shows just what can be done with a small plot. It has an interesting history. In 1922, John Renton and his wife Dorothy bought a plot of land in a select part of Perth – two-thirds of an acre (0.25 ha) of gnarled fruit trees – on which they built a bungalow which filled up most of the space. They decided to buy some of the surrounding land to protect themselves from further possible building development and ended up with 2 acres (0.8 ha) in all. Dorothy Renton was a keen botanist, and she set about making the land into a display garden for her collection of rare plants, often grouping them in island beds so that they could be better viewed. Success followed in 1963 when the Rentons were awarded a First Class Certificate by the Royal Horticultural Society for their poppy-like perennial *Meconopsis grandis* 'Branklyn'. One of Dorothy's great interests was alpine plants, and she demolished a tennis court to build a scree garden which survives today. Sadly, she died in 1966, and two years later, what had become a showpiece among Scottish suburban gardens was deemed interesting enough to be taken over by the National Trust for Scotland.

Since then the garden has been improved and developed and is especially interesting for its alpine plants and rock garden. Among many other plants are rare daphnes and brooms and some fascinating dwarf conifers. Particularly good times to visit the gardens are spring and early summer when the bulbs are in flower, with drifts of snowdrops, snowflakes (*Leucojum vernum*) and trilliums, followed by the rhododendrons, azaleas and magnolias. In the summer there are some unusual hydrangeas in bloom, including *H. involucrata* and *H. sargentiana*. In autumn the blazing red of the maples takes over.

On the eastern side of Perth, off the A85
to Dundee (map page 61)

◆

Left *Bowood's cascade at the north end of the lake*

BRODICK CASTLE   STRATHCLYDE

The castle stands on the north side of Brodick Bay, on the Isle of Arran, and its 60 acres (24 ha) of gardens have been made on ground that slopes steeply to the shore. In the 1920s, the Duchess of Montrose created in a woodland setting what is considered to be one of the finest rhododendron gardens in Europe. Plants from the Himalayas, Burma and China flourish in the gentle west-coast climate and give a continuous display of colour from January to August. There are many other remarkable plants. A *Magnolia campbellii*, capable of reaching 60 ft (18 m), produces warm pink flowers standing erect on leafless branches as early as March, while groups of the evergreen lantern tree (*Crinodendron hookerianum*) have less conspicuous lantern-shaped flowers in April. Originally from Chile, but uncommon in Scotland, is *Nothofagus dombeyi*, which has small dark-green leaves.

Another rarity at Brodick, famous for the resplendent growth it achieves, is a shrubby daisy bush from New Zealand, *Olearia semidentata*, with its distinctive blue flowers and holly-like leaves. During the summer, visit the Walled Garden which has been restored in Victorian style with 'ribbon beds' of annuals, so loved by gardeners in the 19th century. In autumn some rare and colourful hydrangeas take over, backed by the towering columnar shape of *Eucryphia nymansensis*.

On the Isle of Arran, north of the town
of Brodick, on the A841, after travelling
by car ferry from Ardrossan to Brodick
(map page 60)

◆

BURFORD HOUSE GARDEN   SHROPSHIRE

Burford is a good place to visit if you are replanning your garden, for it is a wonderful example of what can be achieved in a relatively short space of time. The gardens cover 4 acres (1.6 ha) and were taken over, together with the Georgian house, by plantsman John Treasure in 1954. At that time they were in an almost derelict state, and most

73

One of the gardens at Capel Manor, designed in a historical style

of the trees and shrubs you see today only date from the 1950s. Mr Treasure's mixture of foliage, flowers and fruit, and his imaginative placing of shapes and colours, will give you plenty of ideas for your own garden; for example, the way that the conifers are set around the pool with vivid red dahlias growing beneath them, or the contrast of the huge leaves of *Gunnera manicata* with the fine golden foliage of *Chamaecyparis obtusa* 'Crippsii'.

There is also an unusual water garden, based on a running stream, as well as a pond. The beds of alpines are also worth viewing, as are the old-fashioned roses. And there are some fine examples of just how a classic herbaceous border can look.

John Treasure is best known, however, for his clematis, and these can be found everywhere. Most of the clematis, together with many other plants from the garden, can be bought here at the large plant nursery which houses the National Collection of Clematis.

Half a mile (1 km) west of Tenbury
Wells, off the A456 (map pages 58–9)

◆

CAPEL MANOR   LONDON

Once the property of the Medcalf family, Capel Manor, a house dating back to the 18th century, is surrounded by a delightful 30-acre (12 ha) garden which looks old, but was in fact mainly replanted over the last ten years or so. There is a horticultural college now in the manor itself and the garden is used for demonstrations. That being so, it is divided into a series of smaller gardens, making it particularly valuable for anyone at the planning stage who is looking for ideas. There is a pool garden, for instance, a woodland area, a walled garden, a herb garden and a knot garden, as well as several other enclosed gardens, bounded by yew hedges, each with their own special theme, including a special area for the disabled with an octagonal greenhouse which has been adapted for the wheelchair-bound. There are also plants for particular places – shade, for example. Alpines are featured, some of them in a glasshouse. Families

of shrubs and plants of special interest tend to be grouped together so they can be compared. A group of magnolias has a ground cover of different geraniums, there is an unusual and important collection of cotoneasters, and you will also find some interesting varieties of sorbus.

There are massed banks of annuals, rose-covered pergolas with hanging baskets of pink geraniums and silver-leaved helichrysum, and an unusual flower bed planted with the bronze-leaved castor oil plant (*Ricinus communis* 'Gibsonii') towering over white- and red-flowered tobacco plants. There are also some magnificent trees, including the tallest copper beech in the country, which is over 200 years old, the second-tallest elm in England, imported from the Caucasus in the 1760s, the Turner oak (*Quercus × turneri*), a semi-evergreen, only shedding its leaves when new growth appears, and a splendid tulip tree (*Liriodendron tulipifera*).

3 miles (5 km) north of Enfield, on the
A10 at the junction with the M25
(map page 59)

◆

CASTLE DROGO   DEVON

This extraordinary 20th-century granite castle stands at over 900 ft (275 m) above sea-level, overlooking the wooded gorge of the River Teign, with stunning views of Dartmoor and the valley below. It was designed by Edwin Lutyens, who also planned the formal flower gardens framed by yew hedges on the slope to the north-east of the castle.

Granite steps lead up to the rectangular enclosed garden with its rose borders and raised paths, where there are all-white flower borders and some splendid shrub roses. In autumn the handsome Persian ironwoods (*Parrotia persica*) in the corners turn amber, crimson and gold. The framework of yew hedges is lined on either side by a serpentine path and herbaceous borders full of old varieties of traditional plants including monkshood, lupins, red hot pokers, campanulas and hollyhocks.

Steps again lead up through a herb garden and shrub borders whose restrained planting is pointed up by some

Continued on page 78

75

Guided Tour

CHATSWORTH DERBYSHIRE

Some of our greatest gardeners have had a hand in developing Chatsworth, and its 105 acres (42 ha) remain as a living history of gardening in Britain over five centuries of change. Its setting in the wooded valley of the River Derwent is magnificent. Above all, it is a memorial to a great friendship between Joseph Paxton, who arrived in 1826 as head gardener, and the 6th Duke of Devonshire.

Outside the orangery, built in 1827, the beds on either side of the path are planted entirely with blue and white annuals, herbaceous plants and 'Iceberg' roses, backed by clipped Irish yews (*Taxus baccata* 'Fastigiata'), while the borders across the Broad Walk which crosses it are in warm oranges, yellows and reds. The Broad Walk itself, backed by golden and green yews, is a third of a mile (0.5 km) long and runs between the Salisbury Lawns and the South Lawn and on through a beech avenue, ending at the top of a rise. At right angles to the Broad Walk is Paxton's Conservative Wall. This series of conservatories, 331 ft (100 m) long, in ascending steps, contains figs, peaches, nectarines and apricots as well as tender shrubs like *Chimonanthus praecox* and *Buddleia auriculata*. In the central portion are two fine *Camellia reticulata* 'Captain Rawes' with trunks 2½ ft (75 cm) in diameter, which were planted in about 1850. In March and April they are covered with huge pink flowers. Opposite, over the steps, is a laburnum tunnel, planted in 1974 and decked in lemon-gold flowers in early June.

Nearby is the modern display greenhouse with a wealth of exotic plants inside. It has three climates: tropical, Mediterranean and temperate. In the tropical section is a pool made for the water-lily *Victoria amazonica* with its giant green leaves with upturned rims. Behind this greenhouse is another more splendid building, the 1st Duke's greenhouse, erected in 1698, which sheltered oranges and myrtles at that time. Now it contains a collection of camellias which always win prizes at the Royal Horticultural Society's spring shows. Before it lies the rose garden with large-flowered roses underplanted with pansies, mallows and lavender. The yews at each end are smothered by climbers and ramblers such as 'Bobbie James', 'Wedding Day' and 'Kiftsgate'.

The rose garden leads to the Salisbury Lawns, created by 'Capability' Brown in the 1760s when he destroyed the formal terraces to make an area of 3 acres (1.2 ha) of grass that he called the Great Slope. They now host innumerable wild flowers and mosses. In his eagerness to make a 'natural' landscape, Brown did away with

CONSERVATIVE WALL

SERPENTINE HEDGE

TEMPLE AND CASCADE

many of the formal features at Chatsworth, but the Cascade escaped his ministrations – a giant water staircase designed by Grillet, a pupil of Le Nôtre. The length of the paving stones over which the water flows and the number and size of individual steps in the 24 groups are all different, so that the sound of the falling water changes.

The rockeries, designed by Paxton, are huge boulders piled on top of one another among conifers and other trees. The grandest of them all, Wellington Rock, is 45 ft (14 m) high with a waterfall which turns into a mass of freezing icicles in winter. On the other side of the path is the Strid Pond, also created by Paxton, and stocked with trout. Further along the wide path is the site of Paxton's vast conservatory, the Great Stove, demolished in the 1920s. This is the place to come in autumn, for a garden has been built within

Chatsworth's gardens contain a wealth of interesting plants and features

part of its foundation walls, featuring flowers like dahlias and Michaelmas daisies. The middle section has a full-sized maze, planted in 1962.

Next comes the Grotto Pond, marked by four big Japanese red cedars (*Cryptomeria japonica*) and, in the far corner, one of the tallest Weymouth pines (*Pinus strobus*) in England. A number of new trees and shrubs have been planted here, including swamp cypresses (*Taxodium distichum*). Behind the pond is the pinetum and arboretum with fine trees.

Nearer the house is the Azalea Dell and

the choice of passing the Ring Pond with its serpentine hedge, or the huge Canal Pond, dug in 1702, with the Emperor Fountain which shoots a jet of water 270 ft (82 m) into the air.

There are two marked routes at Chatsworth: the one with brown arrows covers 1½ miles (2.5 km), while the one with green arrows is half that length. But you really need a day to see this magnificent estate properly.

2 miles (3 km) south of Baslow, off the B6012 (map pages 59–60)

Continued from page 75

fine yuccas at the head of the steps, to culminate in a lovely circular croquet lawn surrounded by high yew hedges, with garden seats designed by Lutyens. Croquet equipment may be hired. On the slopes around the castle itself is a valley of rhododendrons, azaleas and camellias, intermixed with cherries, maples and magnolias. The chapel garden in the shelter of the castle walls is prettily planted with miniature roses, and lavender mixed with box. At the approach to the chapel itself is a huge fig tree, which in most years bears masses of fruit, together with a camellia and a splendid *Garrya elliptica*.

4 miles (6.5 km) south of the A30
Exeter-Okehampton road, off the A382
(map page 58)

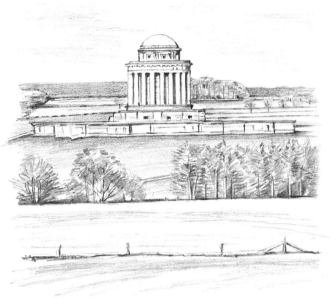

The mausoleum at Castle Howard

CASTLE HOWARD   NORTH YORKSHIRE

This is gardening on an immense scale, with 3000 acres (1200 ha) backed by a further 2000 acres (800 ha) of woodland, and 100 acres (40 ha) of more intimate gardens around the magnificent house, designed by Sir John Vanbrugh. Looking at the scale of the estate, it comes as no surprise to learn that when the park and gardens were developed by the 3rd Earl of Carlisle, Charles Howard, at the beginning of the 18th century, an entire village was demolished to fit in with the grand plan.

You approach the grounds through an imposing 5-mile (8 km) avenue of trees, surrounded by parkland. Straddling the road is Nicholas Hawksmoor's Carrmire Gate, a rubble-built arch with pyramids, towers and turrets. The house is invisible for much of the time, as Vanbrugh was thwarted in his wish to have a straight avenue up to the front by an existing lake. You are beckoned on by a series of obelisks, then, suddenly, the house comes into view. The northern prospect of the house is now dominated by the great lake created in the 1790s. On a ridge on the eastern side, and reached by the Broad Walk, is the ancient Ray Wood, which has been revitalized over the last 15 years and was reopened to the public in 1990. In the spring it is carpeted with primroses, followed by bluebells and foxgloves; here, too, are more than 700 different types of rhododendrons, planted in the 19th century.

To the south, the house now looks out over lawns to the Atlas Fountain, but in the 11-acre (4.4 ha) walled garden, with its flamboyant satyr gate, there are different flower gardens. The rose garden, dedicated to the memory of Lady Cecilia Howard after her death in 1974, houses one of the largest collections of roses in the country. It is planted with a luxuriant mixture of modern and old-fashioned roses, scrambling over attractive trellis cages, interlaced by grass paths, and punctuated by conifers. Some are formally arranged with edgings of box, lavender, and, more unusually, berberis and veronica. The silver-leaved weeping pears and the large plantings of hostas set the vivid flowers off beautifully. In contrast, beyond the wall there is the studied informality of the lake, ponds and New River.

The terrace walk, lined by statues and urns, evolves into a pathway to the Temple of the Four Winds (another Vanbrugh masterpiece), crossing the main street of the now non-existent hamlet of Henderskelfe. From the steps of the temple the landscape unfolds, with the New River bridge, the south lake, the pyramid on the horizon, and the meandering river cascading in a series of waterfalls down into the valley. Lord Carlisle's mausoleum, designed by Hawksmoor, stands isolated, some distance away.

15 miles (24 km) north-east of York, off
the A64, and 6 miles (9.5 km) south-
west of Malton (map page 60)

◆

CHELSEA PHYSIC GARDEN LONDON

In 1673, the Society of Apothecaries of London decided to found a physic garden in Chelsea, at that time a village outside the city and only safely reached by river. Now it remains as a green island protected by buildings from chilling winds, creating a microclimate that enables rare and tender plants to thrive in an urban setting. In the 17th century, plants were the major source of medicines and it was in the physic gardens that physicians and apothecaries were taught how to recognize and use them. The garden is trapezoidal, covering just $3\frac{3}{4}$ acres (1.5 ha), and keeps its original design of narrow rectilinear beds between paths. The plants are set out in systematic order in botanical families – which produces some odd-looking bedfellows. There are also some fine, rare trees including the largest olive grown outdoors in Britain and the magnificent golden rain tree (*Koelreuteria paniculata*).

The oldest rock garden in Europe has rocks of basaltic lava brought from Ireland in 1771 by Joseph Banks; the herb garden contains all the culinary and medicinal plants you can imagine; and the garden holds the National Collection of Cistus. Research and study still continue here – the garden is currently growing feverfew (*Tanacetum parthenium*) for a clinical investigation at King's College into its possible use in treating migraines.

Located in the centre of London at
66 Royal Hospital Road, SW3
(map page 59)

◆

CHENIES MANOR HOUSE BUCKINGHAMSHIRE

The manor house, which dates from the Domesday Survey, has been the scene of many dramas in its time – one of Henry VIII's wives, Catherine Howard, kept a tryst with her lover here which led to her execution in 1542. Henry himself came here too, with Anne Boleyn and the baby Elizabeth I. The gardens at Chenies today have been designed to suit the medieval and Tudor architecture of the house. A large courtyard with wrought-iron gates leads to a small grass maze or labyrinth. There is a large lawn with yews in each corner, surrounded by clipped box, and, in the centre, a stone fountain. The brick wall which serves as a boundary between the gardens and the adjoining churchyard has a mixed shrub and herbaceous border.

The main gardens are divided, in Tudor style, into 'rooms' by hedges and walls. A mixed hedge of cypress and yew trees encloses a narrow path leading to a doorway in the wall at the west end. Beyond this is the physic garden, laid out in formal beds and filled with more than 300 different kinds of herbs. The walls are covered in climbing roses and there is a medieval well. To the north, seen through a screen of ivy-covered trellis, is a rectangular sunken garden, very like the one at HAMPTON COURT PALACE (London), with a series of grassed terraces with 'cushions'

Chenies Manor House, dating from Norman times

of clipped box around a central pond. The beds are full of daffodils and tulips in spring, and herbaceous plants like lady's mantle (*Alchemilla mollis*) in the summer. The sunken garden is separated from the topiary garden by an alley of cypresses and yews surrounding a low central lawn divided by flagstone paths, one of which is lined with clipped box and bounded by pleached limes. In one corner of the sunken garden are the remaining walls of a nursery built in the 16th century for the children of the family. There is also a skittle alley – the beautiful weeping Chinese ash was planted in the 1770s.

The trellis-work arch stretches from the central path to the southern boundary of the garden, and leads to the formal garden whose lawn is decorated with fanciful hens in clipped yew topiary, and a statue of Cupid in the middle. The borders here overflow with bulbs in spring, and later with herbaceous plants. Roses scramble over the wooden trellis-work in summer. On the south side of the garden is a walk of pleached limes forming an arbour overhead, with a mixture of cotoneasters, angelica and holly at their feet. Along the grass path, which is edged by more pleached limes, is a new addition to Chenies: a small white garden.

Between Amersham and
Rickmansworth, north of the A404
(map page 59)

◆

CHIRK CASTLE   CLWYD

Despite its exposed position, standing 700 ft (213 m) above sea-level, picturesque Chirk Castle has a splendid collection of flowering trees and shrubs. Once the gardens consisted of a 'pleasure ground' laid out by Sir Thomas Myddleton, a general in the Civil War. Today, the entrance leads to a fine formal garden with 19th-century topiary yews and hedges giving shelter to a wide range of plants growing by the castle walls, including two unusual honeysuckles, *Lonicera tragophylla* and *L. × brownii*. Beside the second tower lies a group of aromatic shrubs including the orange-barked *Myrtus apiculata*, and jasmine. The rose

garden, to the right, which was laid out at the turn of the century, contains a mixture of floribundas and old hybrid tea varieties like 'Etoile de Hollande' and has a 17th-century sundial as its centrepiece. Further on, the 'crown on cushion' topiary arbour is flanked by beds of musk roses.

A gap in the hedge, guarded by two bronze nymphs, leads to the upper lawn with its 80-yard (73 m) long border of shrubs arranged in successively flowering bays, divided by groups of *Prunus* 'Kanzan'. Opposite are some spectacular trees including silver pendant limes (*Tilia* 'Petiolaris'), willow-leaved magnolias, tulip trees (*Liriodendron tulipifera*) and the Norway maple 'Crimson King'. The lower lawn leads to a rock bank and, nearby, the thatched hawk house, with a collection of camellias behind it. Opposite this is a spectacular shrub garden, in flower mainly in spring and early summer. Here there are some splendid magnolias, ornamental fruit trees, and the handkerchief tree (*Davidia involucrata*) with its curious bracts. There is also a wild garden, bounded by a handsome avenue of limes, planted in the 17th century to provide a vista from the castle. The classical pavilion beyond the ha-ha is an elegant retreat built by William Emes in 1767.

Half a mile (1 km) west of Chirk
village, off the A5 (map page 60)

◆

CHISWICK HOUSE   LONDON

The grounds surrounding this Palladian villa are some of the first examples of William Kent's 'Picturesque' style of gardening. Laid out by Kent and Charles Bridgeman for Lord Burlington from 1727 and influenced by Roman gardens and the Renaissance, they remain formal in layout, with the sombre foliage of cedars and other conifers, sharply clipped yews and a series of stone sphinxes set on funereal plinths, softened only by a meandering canal. Like all gardens of the period there is a wilderness, an early form of shrubbery, and an Italian garden with formal beds. The

Right *Flower borders and yew hedges at Chirk Castle*

amphitheatre-shaped orange-tree garden has a small circular lake with an obelisk in the centre, bounded by orange trees in white tubs. The delightful small Ionic temple is where, it is said, Kent once spent a night watching the effect of the moonlight on his plantings. The camellia house was one of the first conservatories to be built in England, its dome originally decorated in stained-glass panels which made it, according to J.C. Loudon, 'the most gloomy we have seen'. At the time camellias were treated as hothouse plants; now, of course, they are grown outside. The Rustic House has an arched alcove of rusticated stone – an appropriate material for the homes of wood nymphs. On the western side of the house a lawn leads down towards the River – formerly Bollo Brook, a tributary of the Thames which was turned into a canal in the 1700s.

In the centre of London, off Burlington
Lane, W4 (map page 59)

CLAREMONT SURREY

A vast park, with most of its features set well away from the house which has been rebuilt several times, Claremont is the earliest surviving English landscape garden in the romantic style. Begun by Sir John Vanbrugh before 1720, it has had a chequered history, scattered with famous names. It was extended and 'naturalized' by William Kent, then 'Capability' Brown was brought in by the then-owner, Lord Clive of India, to rebuild the house and make some improvements to the grounds – including the diversion of the main London to Portsmouth road to improve a vista.

Claremont boasts two outstanding features: a lake, populated by black swans and surrounded by dense thickets of rhododendrons; and a magnificent amphitheatre, cut in turf, designed by Charles Bridgeman to overlook what was then a round pond but which was later enlarged into a lake by William Kent. There is also a splendid belvedere built in a 'medieval' style by Vanbrugh. The camellia terrace

The amphitheatre at Claremont, from the south of the lake

stands on the site of a camellia house built by Prince Leopold for his wife, Princess Charlotte, who died tragically in childbirth at Claremont. His initial 'L' can be seen on the railings. There is a grotto where parties used to be held – Hugh Walpole described one in 1763: 'The ladies formed a circle of chairs before the mouth of the cave which was overhung to a vast height with woodbines, lilacs and laburnums.'

On the southern edge of Esher, to the
east of the A307 (map page 59)

CLAVERTON MANOR   AVON

A few miles from Bath, situated above the valley of the River Avon, Claverton Manor is now run as the American Museum in Britain. The 15 acres (6 ha) of landscaped grounds also illustrate different aspects of American history: there is a model of an Indian tepee, a covered wagon and the observation platform of a railroad car. Of horticultural interest is the Colonial Herb Garden, complete with straw bee skep, of a scale that could be copied for any suburban plot, and packed full of labelled herbs for cooking, medicine, scent and for making dyes. There is a replica, too, complete with white picket fence, of George Washington's garden at Mount Vernon, Virginia, which was stocked originally with plants and seeds sent from this part of England. Fragrant with roses, it is planted with those varieties of flowers that were popular in America in the 1700s. When Claverton Manor was bought as a museum, it was found to have a number of fine trees of North American origin. These have formed the basis of an American arboretum, fernery and apple orchard, showing how many familiar trees and shrubs we have in common, plus a few surprises like the devil's walking stick (*Aralia spinosa*), the Oregon grape (*Mahonia aquifolium*) and the lodgepole pine (*Pinus contorta latifolia*).

2½ miles (4 km) east of Bath, off the A36
(map pages 58–9)

CLIVEDEN   BUCKINGHAMSHIRE

These are grounds on a grand scale, 130 acres (52 ha) of them with miles of wooded walks, many formal gardens and views of the silvery Thames snaking in the background. Cliveden reached its zenith in Victorian times. It is said that John Fleming, the Duke of Sutherland's gardener who redesigned the great parterre below the house, rebedded the whole of it overnight so that Queen Victoria, who was staying there, could wake up to see a different colour scheme in the morning. It is now planted in a rather more sober vein, with santolina and silvery senecio.

The design of the gardens is dominated, however, by the taste of the Astor family, who donated the property to the National Trust in 1942. The Long Garden, with its exquisite statuary, topiary and clipped box, reflects the 1st Lord Astor's love of Italian Renaissance gardens, as does a balustrade from the forecourt of the Villa Borghese in Rome, which he appropriated to re-erect below the terrace in the 1890s.

The rose garden, with its curved beds echoed in curving, rose-covered arches, was designed on the advice of Geoffrey Jellicoe in 1959, softening the Italianate statues. By the kitchen garden is an intriguing water garden surrounded with acid-loving plants such as azaleas, magnolias and bamboos. The pagoda near the pond was brought from the Great Exhibition in Paris in 1867. The famous flamboyant Fountain of Love stands at the end of the drive up to the house – a huge marble shell with cavorting cupids. There is also a temple, a classical pavilion and a turf amphitheatre. Away from the formality of the gardens surrounding the house, there are splendid woodland walks full of rhododendrons and bluebells in spring.

2 miles (3 km) north of Taplow, on the
B476 (map page 59)

Right *The splendid Forecourt Garden at Cliveden*

Various garden styles are featured at Compton Acres

COMPTON ACRES   DORSET

More a series of display gardens in different styles than an integrated estate, Compton Acres covers 15 acres (6 ha) of sloping land on the top of a cliff on the outskirts of Bournemouth. It was the brainchild of Thomas Simpson, who began work on the gardens after World War I but never finished them. Neglected during World War II, the grounds have been restored and are a popular attraction for both locals and tourists. If you are replanning your garden, then this is the place to come. The grounds contain ten closely-packed sections. There is an Italian garden with a lake, fountains, statues and urns; an English garden with the traditional lawn and herbaceous borders; and a garden of ancient Rome which contains many now rare plants. The Japanese garden is completely authentic, built by a Japanese architect using ornaments and plants imported from Japan and featuring a stone pagoda, a giant heron and some beautiful

Japanese maples. The rock and water garden and the sub-tropical glen are particularly interesting, containing palms, mimosas, jacarandas and other shrubs, and trees not normally grown in our climate, thriving in the shelter of the valley. There is a palm court, a garden of memory, a heather garden and some splendid herbaceous borders, all providing an instructive and highly enjoyable day out.

2 miles (3 km) west of Bournemouth,
on the A35 (map pages 58–9)

◆

CORNWELL MANOR   OXFORDSHIRE

Set in the lush green Oxfordshire countryside, this gracious 17th-century house in Cotswold stone is surrounded by a tranquil, archetypal country house garden of almost 9 acres (3.6 ha) which belies the amount of hard work that has gone into its creation. A nearby stream has been harnessed, for instance, to make canals through the grounds, ending in a series of ponds, one with a superb flight of turfed steps leading to an imposing wrought-iron gate. The water services a bog garden *en route*, which has an attractive collection of plants.

The garden contains a large range of lime-loving plants (such as viburnums, dianthus, hardy geraniums, clematis and lavender), and has something to see at all times of the year. In spring there are drifts of daffodils naturalized under the trees; in summer the terrace balustrades around the house are covered with clematis and roses, and the beds full of peonies, alstroemeria and agapanthus. The garden has an eclectic collection of trees which blend in well with the surroundings. There is a magnificent purple-budded *Magnolia obovata*, a heavily-scented *Osmanthus delavayi*, and the cooler lemon tones of *Hamamelis* 'Pallida' in winter. Weeping pears (*Pyrus salicifolia*) line one of the canals and there is an attractive avenue of cherries, while a sharp, yellow-leaved *Robina pseudoacacia* 'Frisia' contrasts with the grey colouring of an 18th-century dovecote. Look out, too, for *Acer griseum*, the maple with peeling bark showing shiny near-red wood beneath. The paved terrace around the house, edged with catmint (*Nepeta*), is punctuated by a patchwork of ground-cover plants, and white tubs are filled in summer with geraniums, petunias and other half-hardy annuals, as well as the more unusual *Kalmia latifolia*. There is also a secret garden with interesting plants.

2 miles (3 km) west of Chipping
Norton, off the A44 (map page 59)

◆

CRATHES CASTLE GRAMPIAN

Lying in a delightful part of Royal Deeside, Crathes was once the home of the late Sir James and Lady Burnett of Leys, who amassed in their 6 acres (2.4 ha) of sloping ground one of the best collections of trees and shrubs to be found in Britain. Great yew hedges, dating from 1702, surround several of the small gardens, a series of enclosures of which the estate is composed. The croquet lawn leads to the pool garden, which is designed around a square pool with geometric corners of severely clipped topiary, and has plants planned around three colours – red, yellow and purple. The fountain garden, with its statue, a copy of Andrea

A colourful herbaceous border at Crathes Castle

del Verrocchio's *Boy with a Dolphin*, is more formal, and features beds of blue flowers edged by box, offset by columns and domes in yew and holly. The rose garden has a splendid display of floribundas in circular beds, and a border of shrub roses contrasted with hedges of lavender.

The main garden is divided by the wide herbaceous borders flanking narrow flagstone paths, with scarcely a square inch of soil visible. There is a June border featuring many traditional cottage flowers (lupins, irises, poppies, tobacco plants) in pinks, yellows and purples, while the white border has a mixture of white flowers, silver and grey foliage, roses, perennials and flowering shrubs like *Philadelphus microphyllus*. In a lower part of the grounds is the camel garden – the name comes from the shape of the two massive raised beds surrounded by trees and shrubs

3 miles (5 km) east of Banchory, off the
A93 (map page 61)

◆

Crathes Castle has a fine collection of trees and shrubs

The camellia house at Culzean Castle

CULZEAN CASTLE   STRATHCLYDE

Culzean Castle is one of Robert Adam's finest creations, dating largely from 1777. The National Trust for Scotland, who now own it, have an ambitious restoration programme under way. Culzean is particularly notable for its follies and other buildings: the powder house, which stored gunpowder for the Time Gun which was fired from the west green every morning before World War I, the gazebo and the old stable, To the south of the swan pond are the ruins of what once was a splendid pagoda, awaiting restoration. Citrus fruits still grow in their Versailles tubs in the fine orangery which was built in the early 1800s. And the Trust are currently restoring the handsome camellia house which was designed in 1818 by James Donaldson, a pupil of Robert Adam.

In front of the castle lies the fountain garden with terraces and herbaceous borders. There is a walled garden with a large herbaceous border lit by the blazing colour of the red hot pokers (*Kniphofia*) in September. The park, whose 563 acres (225 ha) run down to the shoreline, contains yet more gardens and a woodland walk. There are some fine trees here, brought back by Scottish plant collectors such as Archibald Menzies and David Douglas. Spring at Culzean is marked by the snowdrops which carpet the woodlands, followed by mass displays of bluebells and

Rhododendron arboreum. George Forrest introduced this magnificent species to Britain in about 1810 – the first import from the Himalayas – and it is the parent of many hybrids we see today.

12 miles (19 km) south of Ayr, off the
A719 (map page 60)

◆

DENMANS   WEST SUSSEX

This is a totally modern garden based on plants set in gravel, pebbles and paving. It is a perfect example of easy-care gardening and is full of ideas. This is not surprising since it is managed by designer John Brookes, who is well known for his progressive thinking. The friend of the small gardener, Brookes believes passionately that the garden should be used as an outdoor room. However, the original idea of using gravel came from the garden's owner, Mrs Joyce Robinson, who noticed during a visit to Greece how well plants grew that way on Delos, and came back to make 'dry streams' of gravel.

The $3\frac{1}{2}$ acres (1.4 ha) are planted with easy-care plants like ivy and hostas, which will largely look after themselves. Foliage from blue eucalyptus, yellow yew, red berberis, box and variegated geraniums in pots, is used as much as flowers for dramatic effect. This is seen especially in huge-leaved plants like the giant rhubarb (*Rheum palmatum*). Spikes of mullein and evening primroses, lamium and lavender with lady's mantle (*Alchemilla mollis*) dominate a pretty herb garden, while the wall behind is covered with *Clematis montana rubens*. There are dramatic drifts of plants elsewhere, like Miss Wilmott's ghost (*Erigeron alpinus*) with its blue-green, thistle-like heads, and the giant hogweed towering over it all. There is a pool with yellow lilies, and on the bank the large *Hosta sieboldiana elegans*. An early planting of silver birches and ornamental cherries gives shelter to more tender things. Some plants are from KEW (London) and WISLEY (Surrey); there is an *Arbutus unedo* – the strawberry tree – a liquidambar, a snake-bark maple and a Colorado white spruce. Roses are everywhere, growing

A gravel path leads the way through the fine gardens at Denmans

among herbs and flowering shrubs and spilling over the flint walls, intermixed with clematis.

Near Fontwell, 5 miles (8 km) west of Arundel, on the A27 (map page 59)

DYFFRYN BOTANIC GARDEN
SOUTH GLAMORGAN

This is probably the most famous garden in Wales, designed at the turn of the century by Thomas Mawson for Sir John Cory and his son Reginald – a passionate plant collector who wanted a suitable background in which to display his treasures. There are 55 acres (22 ha) in all, divided up into separate areas, each with a different theme. The large Edwardian mansion, now a conference centre, is surrounded by traditional formal gardens, with flower beds bordered by mature trees and shrubs. There is a croquet lawn, an archery lawn, a paved garden, a rose garden, a herbaceous border and a yew walk. There is also a heather garden, a Roman garden with temple and fountain and, to the side of the house, a well-stocked arboretum and nature reserve, with a collection of birch trees in one corner by the rockery.

Dyffryn's well-tended herbaceous borders are a colour-

South Glamorgan's famous Dyffryn Botanic Garden

ful reminder of how the garden was in its Edwardian heyday. The most impressive feature is the Great Lawn, stretching from the south façade. It is bisected by a splendid canal and lily pond with the newly-restored bronze Dragon Bowl fountain. Other features worth noting include a hedge clipped into the shape of a heart, and a romantic pergola entwined by several different varieties of vine. The huge Temperate House contains plants from all over the world, ranging from citrus trees to a Chinese rice-paper plant. There are other plant houses too, with collections of unusual ornamental plants including orchids, bananas and avocado pears. Another house contains the largest collection of succulents in Wales.

1½ miles (2.5 km) south of St Nicholas, west of Cardiff, off the A48 (map page 58)

EASTGROVE COTTAGE GARDEN
HEREFORD AND WORCESTER

You go back a century or more in time when you enter this enchanting cottage garden, crammed with more than a thousand varieties of traditional plants. A place for plant lovers, the garden surrounds a 17th-century farmhouse and covers three-quarters of an acre (0.3 ha). The garden is sectioned off by paths and hedges with plants spilling over them, and there are roses everywhere. Wide borders are packed with familiar flowers like daisies, poppies and lupins. This is the place to come to learn about colour planting, with some interesting partnerships such as orange and pink, and green and gold foliage. Aromatic shrubs grow here in profusion, rosemary, rue, santolina and sage winding their way among the perennials. Patches of biennials happily seed themselves in odd corners; among them, honesty, foxgloves and forget-me-nots. In contrast to the close-packed flowers, there is a restful area of rough grass punctuated by flowering trees. There is also a bog garden with some beautiful irises and primulas, an alpine garden with tiny plants including saxifrages, and a dwarf conifer bed next

Fine flower borders enhance Eastgrove Cottage Garden

to the patio. There are herbs, of course, and cottage gardener's classics like auriculas. In one corner is a secret garden – romantic with pinks, greys and whites, and shielded by a hedge of the shrubby honeysuckle *Lonicera nitida*. Finally, do not miss the fat topiary duck that stares over a hedge at the bottom of the garden. There is also a hardy plant nursery.

At Sankyn's Green, between Shrawley,
on the B4196, and Great Witley, on the
A443 (map pages 58–9)

◆

EAST LAMBROOK MANOR SOMERSET

So much has been written by, or about, this 'cottage' garden's famous owner – Mrs Margery Fish – that when you visit East Lambrook Manor for the first time the place seems familiar. It is a small garden by visiting standards, but this intimacy is part of its charm. After Mrs Fish's death the garden became overrun and plants (many of them endangered species) disappeared. Now new owners, adhering closely to Mrs Fish's principles, have brought it back to life and have reintroduced the plants that Mrs Fish loved.

Margery Fish was a gifted amateur gardener who learned how to garden the hard way and we can learn a lot from her plantings – in particular her use of ground cover. The gardens surround the old stone house, the malthouse and the cowhouse, with tiny paths snaking among densely planted beds and borders. There is a silver garden, an enclosed area of silver-leaved plants and herbs – dianthus and artemisias, including the common wormwood and *Artemisia absinthium* 'Lambrook Silver'. The back garden wall is covered with climbers and wall shrubs, mainly roses and clematis, but also *Rubus* 'Tridel', cytisus and ceanothus. Look for Mrs Fish's own plants like *Hebe* 'Margery Fish' and *Santolina chamaecyparissus* 'Lambrook Silver'. The famous pudding trees mentioned in her books – bulbous-shaped cypresses – still line a flagstone walk. In late winter and spring the gardens are full of her favourite snowdrops and hellebores; in summer the old apple trees are still covered in climbing roses. You will recognize many of the other plants she loved: primulas in all their infinite varieties, violets, pinks, peonies, tulips and hardy geraniums. The garden is in fact home to one of the National Collections of geranium species.

In East Lambrook, 7 miles (11 km) east
of Ilminster, off the A303
(map page 58)

◆

ERDDIG CLWYD

This large walled garden belongs to what was originally a High Sheriff's house, built in the late 1600s. Two more wings were added in the 18th century and the garden that you see has been restored largely in the style of the early 18th century, reviving several of the features shown in an engraving of the estate in 1739. There are also some 19th-century additions, the parterre for instance, with its 'L'-shaped borders, box hedges and stalagmitic fountains. In its time the house was largely self-supporting: there are niches in the yew hedges where, it is believed, the beehives were kept, the pond was well stocked with fish, and they produced their own vegetables and fruit. In 1975 the main

A lovely pink Hydrangea petiolaris *climbs a wall at Erddig*

garden was replanted with fruit trees, following wherever possible existing lists of 1718. The names are mouthwatering: Spanish Musk Pare, Orange Apricock and White Mogull, for example, some of them trained in espaliers and fans against the old walls. Some of these varieties are served in the restaurant and are sometimes on sale. As well as this unique collection of ancient fruit varieties, the garden walls support an interesting collection of climbers including clematis, *Hydrangea petiolaris* and roses. Beneath them grow a range of summer-flowering plants and a collection of rare old daffodils and narcissi.

From the handsome 18th-century wrought-iron screen in the wall at the end of the long canal there is a view of the house through an avenue of pleached limes. The canal walk is edged in spring and early summer by wild bulbs like narcissi and fritillaries, and decorated with Portuguese laurels grown in wooden Versailles tubs. Beside a shady spinney lies the Victorian garden with roses in stone-edged beds mixed with clematis and underplanted with thrift, London pride, catmint and agapanthus. There is an avenue of wellingtonias and monkey puzzle trees much loved by the Victorians, and the National Collection of Ivies is grown here. More fruit decorates the garden, medlars and damsons grow beyond the boundaries of the walled garden, cherry trees line the car park and, on the wall above a border of herbs, a fig tree flourishes. In a dell below the house is a curiosity: the Cup and Saucer which once supplied water to the house. Water from a nearby brook flows into a circular basin with a cylindrical waterfall at its centre, then emerges from a tunnel. Nearby is an ingenious late 19th-century hydraulic ram which pumps water up to the house.

2 miles (3 km) south of Wrexham, off
the A525 (map page 60)

◆

EXBURY GARDENS   HAMPSHIRE

This splendid 250-acre (100 ha) estate, situated on a narrow peninsula between the Solent and the Beaulieu River, contains a collection of over a million rhododendrons and azaleas, spread over three areas: Home Wood, where the earliest flowering shrubs are, stretches down towards the Beaulieu River to the south-west of the house; Witcher's Wood is named after a local gypsy family; and Yard Wood is linked to the rest of the estate by a white balustraded bridge over Gilbury Lane. In the depths of this wood is a gnarled old yew tree that is reputed to have been recorded in the Domesday Survey, and Yard Wood is so-called because its yews provided the bows for the Norman and Plantagenet kings.

Exbury was planted by Lionel de Rothschild, who

bought the property in 1919 when it formed part of the New Forest, and it remains in the family today. During his lifetime Mr de Rothschild raised many plants from seed collected for him on expeditions to the Himalayas, China and Japan. He also bred over a thousand new hybrid rhododendrons and azaleas of which nearly 500 were actually registered as new varieties. Look for the beautiful pink-flowered 'Naomi', named after his youngest daughter, near Lovers' Lane in Witcher's Wood, and the unusual yellow 'Hawk Crest' by the main crossroads.

However, there is more to see at Exbury than simply rhododendrons, for there are some magnificent specimens of magnolias and camellias as well. Although Exbury is at its best in spring and early summer, many unusual trees come into their own when the rhododendrons have finished flowering: the huge swamp cypress (*Taxodium distichum*), for instance, which dominates the island on the upper pond, and the weeping Brewer spruce (*Picea brewerana*), as well as the handsome oaks and the Scots pines. On hot summer days the rose garden, planted in memory of the late Lady Rothschild, is filled with beautiful blooms. The present owner, Edmund de Rothschild, has restored and replanted the 2-acre (0.8 ha) rock garden, once built with the aid of a crane and which now shows off some stunning dwarf azaleas. He has himself bred some new varieties of rhododendron, notably the 'Solent' varieties which edge the long avenue called Lovers' Lane.

**Between Beaulieu and Dibden Purlieu,
off the B3054 (map page 59)**

◆

FALKLAND PALACE FIFE

Falkland Palace, with its royal tennis court, was built in the 1500s, when it became the country sporting residence of the Stewart kings and queens, notably Mary Queen of Scots. In its early days it seems that the 11-acre (4.4 ha) gardens were used rather to provide food and herbs than for pleasure. During World War II they were turned temporarily into a nursery for forest trees. Soon afterwards,

however, the Keeper of the Palace appointed Percy Cane, the well-known landscape architect, to design gardens appropriate to the historic palace. Cane extended the relatively small area which had been gardened and positioned beds and borders to create a circular walk around the outer limits of the lawn.

Near the palace, pastel or often white flowers are used, in order not to detract from the buildings themselves. In the foundations of a ruined building is a formal rose garden, where red and yellow roses are used to great effect, backed by silver foliage. There is a pink and blue border on the ground sloping from the sturdy outer walls, with plants like *Erigeron* 'Quakeress'. Alstroemerias mingle with shrub roses in one corner of the garden, and a grassed North Walk has an astrolabe as its focal point. The herb garden is set out as an amusing chequers game. April and May are good months to visit, when the cherry blossom is out.

**11 miles (17.5 km) north of Kirkcaldy,
on the A912 (map page 61)**

◆

FARNBOROUGH HALL WARWICKSHIRE

A visit to Farnborough Hall, which has been home to the same family since 1684, will give you a fascinating glimpse of what life must have been like for a country landowner in the 18th century. It was owned at that time by William Holbech, who returned from a fashionable Grand Tour of Europe much influenced by the landscape architecture he had seen in France and Italy. In 1745 he set to work, with a friend and neighbour Sanderson Millar, landscaping his 160-acre (64 ha) park, creating grandiose vistas, an obelisk, and temples in the classic style. First he made a sequence of four pools to the west and north of the Hall, and a pretty oval temple, used as a summerhouse, from which there were splendid views. All these remain today, together with fascinating domestic buildings such as the hexagonal game larder overlooking ponds and lakes. But Squire Holbech's most impressive piece of work is the secluded grassed terrace walk, some 40 ft (12 m) wide, with

An obelisk stands at the south end of the Serpentine Terrace at Farnborough Hall

two temples, curving for three-quarters of a mile (1 km) between Farnborough Hall and an estate at Mollington, where his brother lived. From the terrace there are fine views across the rolling countryside to the Malvern Hills across the valley and, nearer to hand, Edge Hill, the Civil War battlefield. There are additional delights such as the pretty rose garden with an arbour let into the brick wall and painted to match the pink of 'The Fairy' rose that surrounds it.

6 miles (9.5 km) north of Banbury, off the A423 (map page 59)

◆

GARSINGTON MANOR   OXFORDSHIRE

This garden is the creation of the late Lady Ottoline Morrell, the bohemian socialite who came to the little village of Garsington in the 1920s, and proceeded to stamp her personality on it. Writing later in her memoirs, Lady Ottoline said that she sometimes felt as if their house and garden were a theatre where 'week after week a travelling company would arrive and play their parts', and certainly

Garsington Manor – now being extensively replanted

the garden has a lingering feel of those pre-World War II days about it, when house parties included Aldous Huxley, Lytton Strachey, Charlie Chaplin, Prime Minister Lord Asquith and the novelist Katharine Mansfield.

The Jacobean house, festooned with climbing roses and with an old pear tree growing against it, has a forecourt enclosed by stone gates and dark walls of yew. A formal box and flower parterre has its box-edged sections filled with scarlet tulips in spring. In spring, too, cherry blossom cascades over a flight of turfed stone steps, and fastigiate clipped yews stand to attention. A series of grass terraces descend to ponds with crumbling Italian statues and cypresses, which give an Italian touch. In Lady Ottoline's day, peacocks spread their tails to a backdrop of dark green yews and walked along the grass paths. The present owners allow a local dramatic group to present plays on the lawn, and opera productions are staged in summer on the stone loggia. They have also built a new garden in a former paddock, and are undertaking extensive replanting and restoration.

4 miles (6.5 km) south-east of Oxford, off the B480 (map page 59)

◆

GRAYTHWAITE HALL GARDENS   CUMBRIA

The Victorian landscape architect Thomas Mawson laid out these 12-acre (5 ha) gardens in the early 1890s, and went on to become an international success. The house, which dates from the 16th century but now has a Victorian façade, nestles in what was a gloomy hollow. Mawson, however, completely altered the landscape, taking out large numbers of mature trees, and clearing the high ground on the western side to let in more light. He then went on to change the course of the stream which ran through the grounds, giving it a serpentine route with cascades at intervals. Today it acts as a natural division between the lawn to the south of the house and the woodland garden in which rhododendrons and azaleas, which do so well in this part of the country, are densely planted – look for *Rhododendron hunnewellianum hemsleyanum* with scented white flowers, and *R. litiense* and *R. hunnewellianum* 'Butterfly' with yellow flowers. Like many gardens of that era, it has formal planting around the house, then a looser, freer design below.

A great deal of Mawson's work remains, a triumph in dealing with what is basically a thin layer of soil over solid rock. His Dutch garden is just as it was when he planted it, enclosed by clipped yew hedges. Inside it are box-edged beds filled first with spring bulbs and polyanthus, then summer annuals. The wrought-iron gates guarded by cherubs were made by Mawson's architect friend Dan Gibson, who was also responsible for the sundial in the centre of the rose garden. For the best view over the garden, and the way it was planned, stand in front of the summerhouse, close to the Dutch garden.

4 miles (6.5 km) north of Newby Bridge
on the west side of Lake Windermere
(map page 60)

Great Dixter, the home of author Christopher Lloyd

GREAT DIXTER   EAST SUSSEX

Great Dixter, one of the 20th century's most outstanding gardens, will already be familiar to many, through the pages of plantsman and writer Christopher Lloyd's own books. In the early 1900s, the Lloyd family employed Edwin Lutyens to restore the original 15th-century house and farm buildings, and lay out formal gardens in the 5 acres (2 ha) around it. Lutyens is largely responsible for the interlacing steps, walls and gateways that link the levels of the garden together, and the brick arches in the walled garden that lead to the sunken garden and to the lawn below. Nathaniel Lloyd, author of *Garden Craftsmanship in Box and Yew*, made the many enclosures in the garden, using yew hedging to provide protection for tender plants. In doing so, he gave the garden an air of intimacy, providing an attractive foil for the largely cottage garden plants inside. The main lawn is decorated by topiary with shapes set like chess pieces, and there is a separate topiary garden where giant birds sit on conical plinths of yew.

There is so much to see at Great Dixter. Be sure to visit the sunken pool, designed by Nathaniel Lloyd, with its raised beds around it, the old vegetable garden, the walled garden, the rose garden, and, of course, the famous long herbaceous border over 200 ft (60 m) in length, 15 ft (4.5 m) wide, edged by a flagstone path. Great Dixter is a living lesson in planting for all-year-round interest. The orchard, for example, is underplanted with fritillaries, wild orchids, anemones and autumn crocuses, each coming out in turn. The wild-flower meadow, too, is one of the best in England. Each year there is something new to see as the garden continually evolves under Christopher Lloyd's care.

Near Northiam, 12 miles (19 km) north
of Hastings, on the A28 (map page 59)

HADDON HALL   DERBYSHIRE

Roses are a speciality of Haddon Hall. They clothe the walls of the castellated house and decorate most of the garden: floribundas, shrub roses, climbers and hybrid teas,

Haddon Hall, with roses surrounding the leaded windows

often mixed with *Clematis* 'Jackmanii'. They also cover the thick buttressed walls which support the terraced gardens. Haddon even has a special rose of its own, 'Mary Manners', named after Lady John Manners. This is the place to see some unusual half-forgotten varieties of climber such as *Rosa kordesii* 'Dortmund', 'Colonel Pool', and 'Parkdirektor Riggers'.

Parts of the ancient 6-acre (2.4 ha) gardens of Haddon Hall, carved out of a limestone hill, may well date back to the 12th century, the time when the house was built, but the main structure dates from the 1800s. There are three terraces behind the house. The top one, edged by a magnificent balustrade, has been in turn a bowling green, a winter garden, and now a rose garden, with neat lawns and two very old yews. Visit the gardens in April and May for spring bulbs, in June to see the early clematis and the early climbing roses. In July and August there are more roses, a magnificent display of delphiniums and a fine herbaceous border, and September brings the late-flowering climbers and autumn colour.

South-east of Bakewell, on the A6
(map pages 59–60)

◆

HAMPTON COURT PALACE   LONDON

Hampton Court's gardens have been popular since they were first opened to the public by Queen Victoria in 1838. Built for Cardinal Wolsey in the 1500s, the first grand gardens in England, and annexed by Henry VIII who preferred to build bowling alleys and a tiltyard, the gardens at Hampton Court really came into their own when the famous maze was built in 1714. But they date from many periods. The splendid fountain garden, a complicated *parterre de broderie* adorned with statues and 13 fountains, was designed for William and Mary by a Huguenot refugee, Daniel Marot. Queen Anne swept most of this away, and in the 19th century the garden was used for displays of bedding plants. Charles II built the Long Water with its radiating lime avenues, in imitation of the canal at the Palace

The pond gardens at Hampton Court Palace

of Versailles. The huge cones of clipped yew survive from the 17th century, and along the Broad Walk is a splendid 20th-century herbaceous border 1000 ft (300 m) long, while modern planting now adorns the pond gardens by the banqueting house.

The 16th-century privy garden with its grass paths is stocked with mainly 19th-century shrubs. Do not miss the wilderness, or the tiltyard with its observation towers – now a rose garden. The famous great vine, bearing black Hamburg grapes, was planted at Hampton Court during the time of 'Capability' Brown, master gardener at the palace in the 1700s. The Tudor knot garden was reconstructed in 1924, for little of the original plantings remained. And there is a priory garden, filled with flowers, statues, lawns and a fountain, from which you can view the Thames through an elaborate wrought-iron screen.

To the east of East Molesey, on the
A308 at the junction with the A309
(map page 59)

◆

HARDWICK HALL   DERBYSHIRE

Built as a hunting lodge for Bess of Hardwick in the 16th century, the 7½-acre (3 ha) grounds of Hardwick Hall were laid out as formal enclosed gardens at the time. But

Continued on page 102

A flower border in orange and yellow brightens a wall at Hardwick Hall

Guided Tour

◆

HATFIELD HOUSE
HERTFORDSHIRE

When the old Palace of Hatfield was built in 1497, the gardens would certainly have included knots, herbers and possibly a privy garden. Later when Robert Cecil, 1st Earl of Salisbury, built Hatfield House itself, there were water parterres, grass knots, mounts and elabor-ate fountains. But all this was swept away in the landscape revolution of the 18th century, when the parkland was brought up to the very walls of the house. Now the original gardens are making their return, for since the 19th century the Salisburys have been redesigning gardens round the house and palace, restoring them to their former formal splendour.

The present Marchioness, in particular, has taken on the task with enthusiasm, introducing new plantings to complement the buildings; the lower West Garden, for instance, now has a scented garden with a herb garden at its centre, and a knot garden has been made in the courtyard of the Old Palace.

You enter the gardens on the north side of Hatfield House. Immediately on your left is a broad bed filled with shade-loving plants, among them *Lamium galeobdolon* with its silver-marked leaves and yellow flowers, under the shelter of two *Phillyrea latifolia*. At the T-junction of the box-edged paths, turn left into the pleached lime walk with a narrow brick-

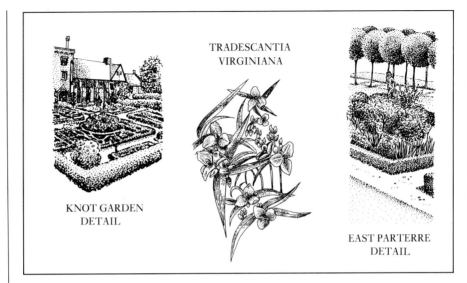

KNOT GARDEN
DETAIL

TRADESCANTIA
VIRGINIANA

EAST PARTERRE
DETAIL

edged border planted with spring flowers which come out before the leaves of the limes and so get the light they need. Turn right on to the lawn of the privy garden and you will find an entrance in the low, undulating yew hedge that takes you into the central flower garden. This garden was made by Lady Gwendolen Cecil in 1899–1900, copying a design she found in the archives. Many old-fashioned roses are in bloom there in summer, notably *Rosa chinensis* 'Bloomfield Abundance' with its creamy pink flowers. There are poppies, too, and lupins and lilies. There are also more than a hundred different pinks, violas and pansies. Later in the season the cosmos and Michaelmas daisies appear, also clumps of phlox. In the north-west corner hedge of the parterre, by the stone seat, is a large old mulberry (*Morus nigra*), the sole survivor of four planted by James I.

Leave the parterre by the southern exit and go into the wilderness garden via a flight of cobbled steps and wander through the 13 acres (5 ha) of trees and shrubs, some of which have spectacular colour in autumn – for example, the *Parrotia persica*, *Prunus sargentii* and *Malus tschonoskii*. Retracing your steps along one of the mown grass paths to the *rondpoint* with its stone urn, you will come to the holly walk, a broad grass *allée* flanked on either side by high holly hedges. This leads through a wrought-iron gate to the scented garden. On your right is a sheltered corner for tender plants such as Carolina allspice (*Calycanthus floridus*), an

Part of the Old Palace garden

aromatic shrub from North America, and *Jasminium officinale*. The paved path on the right is hedged with the heavily-scented Guernsey stock, while the path on the left leads to a seat turfed in camomile and enclosed by clipped box, where you can sit and smell the heady perfume of *Lilium regale*, *Rosa* 'Souvenir du Docteur Jamain', and the many scented violas and dianthus.

In the centre of the scented garden, among paths planted with camomile, is the herb garden, designed around a sundial and surrounded by a hedge of sweet briar. The four main beds are edged with the dwarf Munstead lavender, and old-fashioned centifolia roses grow among the herbs. From the north-east corner take a flight of steps back to the lime walk and, half-way down, turn left and you can see the knot garden. Here the Marchioness has made three knots, and a foot maze, or labyrinth, around a central fountain. The

knots are filled with plants dating from the 15th, 16th and 17th centuries. Here, in circular beds, are two clipped variegated hollies, one gold and green, the other silver and green.

Planted in the knots, too, is a collection of plants known to have been grown in the gardens at Hatfield by John Tradescant the Elder when he was employed to plant and lay out the gardens for Robert Cecil, 1st Earl of Salisbury, in the early 17th century. Some of these plants Tradescant brought back from abroad; others, from the New World, were brought back by his son. Of particular interest is the double peony, given to Tradescant by the Emperor Maximilian's gardener, and *Tradescantia virginiana*, with its curious three-petalled flower, brought back by his son from Virginia.

Opposite Hatfield railway station, on the A1000 (map page 59)

Continued from page 98

most of the design and planting you see today dates from relatively recent times. The garden in the forecourt has a neat geometrical arrangement of beds and lawns, backed by cedar trees, while on the east side of the house is a lawn dominated by a circular pond. The hedge beyond has a gap in it revealing a ha-ha behind it and parkland beyond. Enter the house, and from the east windows you can view an unusual planting of limes in the park beyond, forming the shape of an upturned goblet. The main garden, to the south, is divided into four sections by two splendid alleys of hornbeam hedges running east to west, crossed by yew hedges running north to south. Where they meet in the centre is a hidden garden with seats and statues. Each quarter is treated differently: one is a lawn, dominated by Hungarian oaks (*Quercus frainetto*), with borders of roses and herbaceous plants; the two eastern quarters are orchards, one ancient and filled with gnarled old apple trees, borders of shrub roses, a row of mulberries and a wild-flower lawn, the other containing a modern orchard planted with old varieties of fruit.

One of the main attractions at Hardwick Hall is a splendid 'Elizabethan' herb garden laid out in the old vegetable garden. Planted in the 1970s, it contains mainly plants known before 1700, in beds edged with lavender, punctuated with cones of golden hops scrambling over metal frames, and with hedges of eglantine roses and sweetbriar. Also at Hardwick Hall is a nuttery and, in May, a colony of lilies-of-the-valley in flower, their leaves edged in white.

6½ miles (10 km) north-west of Mansfield,
off the A617 (map pages 59–60)

◆

HEVER CASTLE   KENT

This perfect little 13th-century castle (actually a manor house), complete with moat, portcullis and drawbridge, was the childhood home of Anne Boleyn. The 30-acre (12 ha) gardens that go with it, despite their ancient look, were created almost entirely by the American millionaire William Waldorf Astor between 1904 and 1908. He

The pergola walk at Hever Castle

employed over a thousand men to work on the design, digging out a 35-acre (14 ha) lake in the process. In 1906 he bought a vast number of pieces of topiary and planted the perfectly-kept 80 ft (24 m) square maze which now reaches 8 ft (2.5 m) in height. It has the initials 'H' and 'A' for Henry and Anne cut in a clipped box medallion in front of it. Alongside the maze is Anne Boleyn's Garden, laid out as it might have been in her time as a series of small gardens. There is a Tudor herb plot and a paved fountain garden, planted with white 'Yvonne Rabier' roses and 'Sander's White Rambler' standards in the corner. The chess garden has some spectacular chessmen clipped from golden yew, modelled on figures dating from Henry VIII's reign that Astor saw in the British Museum.

Opposite the entrance to the castle, a bridge leads over the outer moat towards the 5-acre (2 ha) Italian garden packed full of antiquities bought by William Astor when he was American Minister in Rome, and shipped to Hever. The garden houses a splendid collection of classical sculpture set off by brilliantly coloured beds of flowers, flowering shrubs and roses. In the centre is a hedged sunken garden with a pool and borders of flowers. There is a Pompeian

Right *Antique terracotta jars at Hever Castle*

wall which stretches for an eighth of a mile (0.2 km) and is decorated with more statues and urns almost enveloped by shrubs and climbers, plus a splendid pergola along the south wall, intertwined with wisteria and roses and supported by laburnum and apple trees. Astor also added an Italianate loggia, designed by Frank Pearson, from which there are stunning views over the lake. Beyond the confines of the moat there are informal plantings of shrubs and ornamental trees which extend beside the Golden Stairs. Finally, Anne Boleyn's Walk, a 500-yard (457 m) grassed ride edged with trees, forms the southern boundary to the estate from where you have a view back to the castle and its surroundings. Across the moat behind the castle there is a surprise: a complete 'Tudor village'.

3 miles (5 km) south-east of
Edenbridge, off the B2026
(map page 59)

Hidcote Manor Garden   GLOUCESTERSHIRE

It was an American landscape architect and keen plant collector, Major Lawrence Johnston, who created this beautiful garden from 10 acres (4 ha) of windswept farm fields and an unyielding clay soil, at the turn of the century. Photographs taken at that time, on display near the entrance, give some idea of the problems he faced. Today it is still a reference point for most gardeners, and one of the most constantly quoted gardens in this country. When Major Johnston took over the plot in 1907, it had nothing but one fine cedar of Lebanon and two clumps of beeches to its credit. It took him 40 years to complete the task and see the results of his planning and planting come to fruition.

The central feature at Hidcote is the path which leads you through a series of interlocking hedge-lined outdoor rooms, a series of secret gardens – more than 20 in all – each with a different theme and luxuriant with plants. The red border, a vivid, at times clashing mixture of bronzes, reds and purples, has trees such as the purple-leaved plum and purple-leaved hazel, with red lobelia and scarlet dahlias

growing beneath them. There is a white garden, a holly walk and a pool garden with a central fountain, water-lilies and fish. The rose garden has a superb collection of old-fashioned roses, and there is an unusual stilt garden featuring clipped pleached hornbeams on stems. A pillar garden has tall columns of yew and borders of 'Hidcote' lavender, while the kitchen garden has been turned into an Old Rose walk. Mrs Winthrop's Garden, named after Major Johnston's mother, is paved and has a blue and yellow theme, with pale lime, beech and hornbeam hedges. In the fuchsia garden, plants are coralled in neat box edging. There is a stream garden, too, fringed by marsh-loving plants. The theatre lawn is the largest area, enclosed by yew hedges, with a single stately beech on the 'stage' which is carpeted with spring bulbs in the early months of the year. Major Johnston is said to have created the idea of a 'tapestry' hedge; at Hidcote there are hedges containing a mixture of native shrubs such as beech, box and yew, giving you a chance to see just how attractive the idea can be.

3 miles (5 km) north-east of Chipping
Campden, off the B4081 (map page 59)

Hill Top   CUMBRIA

When author and artist Beatrix Potter, famed for her children's books, bought Hill Top in 1905 with its $1\frac{1}{2}$ acres (0.6 ha), she felt she had finally moved into her dream cottage. She was 46 at the time, and had purchased the property with money earned from her books. It was her first garden, and she took to it with great enthusiasm, begging seeds, plants and cuttings from all her neighbours. 'I think I have had something out of nearly every garden in the village,' she wrote to a friend. At first she only used it as a holiday home; later, when she married and went to live nearby, it became her own secret place, somewhere to write, to paint and to entertain. She even kept a pet pig there, called Sally, who used to follow her about.

Right *Peonies in the pillar garden at Hidcote Manor*

Beatrix Potter was determined to create the archetypal romantic cottage garden and succeeded, and it became the inspiration for several of her books and can be seen in many of her paintings.

Today it is just as pretty: bleeding heart, dianthus, peony and iris, all the cottage flowers, decorate the flower beds, together with hollyhocks, mulleins and lady's mantle. And a pink-flowered enkianthus somehow survives the winters here. The border leading up to the house is straight out of Tom Kitten with its canterbury bells, snapdragons and pansies, with spikes of mullein and foxgloves, and there is sage and onion for the Gentleman with Sandy Whiskers. In spring there are daffodils, of course, and in summer old-fashioned roses such as 'Albéric Barbier', 'American Pillar' and 'Leverkusen', with white wisteria, and a porch with honeysuckle and heavily-scented roses. There is rosemary for remembrance, clematis in great quantity, and great umbels of angelica. And in winter the Japanese quince (*Chaenomeles japonica*) is particularly colourful.

Beatrix Potter's cottage became a place of pilgrimage even before she died in 1943, so she kept a rabbit in a hutch so that children asking for Peter Rabbit would not be disappointed. Her ashes are scattered on the hill beyond the house. A new vegetable garden has been planted and a charming touch, today, is the egg which is religiously kept in Jemima Puddleduck's rhubarb patch for all the young visitors to find.

Near Far Sawrey on the western side of
Lake Windermere, on the B5285
(map page 60)

———————◆———————

HOLKER HALL   CUMBRIA

Holker Hall, which lies on low ground close to the west coast of Cumbria, is surrounded by a splendid 200-acre (80 ha) park, 18th-century in origin. Beside this there are 20 acres (8 ha) of gardens which have been worked by generations of the Cavendish family, cousins of the Dukes of Devonshire, who still live here. Although part of the house dates from the 16th century, it falls into two sections, the main part of which is Victorian, rebuilt by the Duke of Devonshire after a disastrous fire in 1871. To the north and west are wooded slopes. The oldest part of the garden can be found just below the paved terrace, on the south side of the house. Here the ground is divided into four by mature yew hedges, with columnar Irish yews standing to attention alongside the steps. There are some splendid herbaceous borders, and one which features an attractive combination of peonies and old-fashioned shrub roses. In late spring, dwarf Japanese rhododendrons are in flower. To the west of the house there is a garden guarded by hedges of clipped hornbeam with alcoves in which are displayed marble busts. To the south of the old part of the house there is another formal garden edged by beech hedges and mainly shrub borders. The wrought-iron pillars and arbours have young clematis, honeysuckle and roses twining over them. From some of the gardens there are splendid views to Morecambe Bay.

The woodland garden, in contrast to all the formality, is more open in character, with grassy slopes covered in spring with bulbs and wild flowers including bluebells; there are also mature trees, rhododendrons and azaleas. The best times for the magnificent flowering trees and shrubs (the acers, eucryphias and pieris) are spring and early summer, and again in the autumn. There is also a monkey puzzle tree, which was planted by Joseph Paxton, the designer of Crystal Palace, and has survived against all odds. When, towards the end of the 19th century, it was blown over during a storm, it was pulled up by a team of seven shire horses, then bedded down in cement and stones, and remarkably continues to flourish today. The garden has a walled boundary on the northern side, against which many shrubs, including several magnolias, are grown. A cedar of Lebanon remains, the last of five grown from seed sent to Lord George Cavendish from the Holy Land.

Formality creeps in again with the pool and fountain, with stone steps leading to a statue of Neptune and a newly-restored sunken rose garden. New things are happening here all the time: there is a new rose garden and a limestone cascade. Blessed with a warm microclimate, thanks to the nearby Gulf Stream, plants grow apace. But the woodland walks will always be the main reason to come here.

4 miles (6.5 km) south-west of
Grange-over-Sands, on the B52878
(map page 60)

HOLKHAM HALL NORFOLK

You feel as if you have stepped back in time to the 18th century when you view the majestic sweep of Holkham Hall's landscape. And that, in effect, is what you are doing, for this fine estate is almost perfectly preserved from that time. There is a park, with deer, an area of woodland, and farmland, covering in all over 3000 acres (1200 ha). William Kent was responsible for both the park and the Palladian Hall, built for Thomas Coke, 1st Earl of Leicester. (Coke had met Kent while on the Grand Tour.) Kent reclaimed a marshy inlet to make the Great Lake to the west of the house, and built the classical temple, the triumphal arch and the obelisk. Later, under the 2nd Earl, 'Coke of Norfolk', 'Capability' Brown's pupil William Emes and Humphry Repton each had a hand in the park's design.

The formal terraces and parterres around the house

Kent's classical temple at Holkham Hall

were constructed in the 19th century by W.A. Nesfield, as was the George and Dragon fountain. There is a 6-acre (2.4 ha) walled garden which contains the original greenhouses, and the oldest building in the park is a fascinating tepee-shaped ice house near the southern end of the lake. The mature trees that form such a feature of the estate are gradually being added to by the present Viscount Coke to ensure that the landscape will remain essentially the same in years to come.

2 miles (3 km) west of Wells-next-the-
Sea, on the A149 (map page 59)

HOWICK HALL NORTHUMBERLAND

In sharp contrast to the wild and windswept Northumberland coast with its fortresses, Howick Hall, with its sheltered microclimate, is a haven where many exotic and rare plants can be found. It is the home of the Grey family, and Lord Grey, a member of the Whig Government in the 1830s, retired to Howick when his party fell from power at the time of the Napoleonic wars. During his time in the political wilderness, he set to work on the gardens and planted a large number of trees, which survive to this day. In the 19th century the gardens of Howick consisted mainly of terraces around the house, descending to a valley with a stream running through it. Today they have some splendid borders of showy agapanthus, herbaceous plants and roses. There is also a rare variety of *Clematis montana* growing below the corner of the top terrace. On one side is a meadow planted profusely with bulbs, flowering not just in spring but in autumn too, with ox-eye daisies growing in the months between. There is also a handsome golden oak, a handkerchief tree (*Davidia involucrata*), and a yew hedge fronted by red hot pokers in summer.

Lord Grey's happy discovery in the 1930s of a pocket of 4 acres (1.6 ha) of acid soil, in what was normally limestone, has led to the making of Silverwood, a woodland garden beyond the meadow. It is (unexpectedly in this limestone region) full of acid-loving plants: there are

rhododendrons and azaleas grown from seed collected on expeditions to Asia before World War II, cherries and camellias, some spectacular magnolias up to 40 ft (12 m) tall, and acers and cercidiphyllums with their splendid autumn colour. The woodland garden also gives shelter to tender plants such as the Chilean firebush (*Embothrium lanceolatum*) with its scarlet clusters of flowers, and the paths through the wood are edged with primulas. Howick Hall also has a rare collection of wild plants, some of which have been grown from seed collected in North America. At the moment, an arboretum is being planted to the west, north and east of the garden, which is partly to replace a canopy of old beeches and other broad-leaved trees which are nearing the end of their life.

6 miles (9.5 km) north-east of Alnwick,
off the B1339 (map page 60)

IFORD MANOR   WILTSHIRE

In a spectacular setting overlooking the valley of the River Frome, and not far from Bradford on Avon, is Iford Manor, sheltered by a backdrop of woodland, with its terraced gardens above it and to the side. This house was owned in the early 1900s by Harold Peto, a disciple of the Arts and Crafts movement. Peto fell in love with classical Italian architecture and landscaping, and decided to emulate them in England, even down to the tall cypress trees. After an extended tour of Italy, he brought home countless statues and huge pots, and commissioned copies of others, dotting them all around the garden.

Paths of gravel and flagstones, edged with plants such as lady's mantle and iris, lead from one area to another. It is a garden strong on statuary, attractive local stone, and water features, punctuated with juniper, box, yew and the cypresses. In contrast to all this there is an attractive flower meadow of bulbs naturalized in grass, including martagon lilies as well as the more usual bulbous plants. Terraced

A view of the Great Terrace at Iford Manor

Continued on page 112

109

Guided Tour

◆

INVEREWE GARDEN HIGHLAND
Behind this garden in the heart of the Highlands lies the story of one man's persistence in making a romantic retreat in the middle of barren heathland. When Osgood Mackenzie came to Inverewe in 1862, the only tree that existed was a stunted willow about 3 ft (less than 1 m) high. He set to work, planting hundreds of Scots and Corsican pines to provide shelter for the woodland garden of sub-tropical shrubs which were added later. As a result, if you now come to Inverewe in spring or early summer you can see the finest specimen in Britain of the brilliant magenta-flowered *Rhododendron hodgsonii*, and alongside it the equally impressive *Rhododendron sinogrande* from Tibet,

with its cream to canary-yellow blooms. But pride of place probably goes to a magnificent *Magnolia campbellii* more than 40 ft (12 m) high, with pink flowers as large as dinner plates in March and April. Growing in the shade of these magnificent shrubs is the true Himalayan poppy, *Meconopsis betonicifolia*, in drifts of vivid blue. Another group of plants to look out for are the candelabra primulas, standing taller than the usual variety. They flower in late May and June and range in colour from the red *Primula japonica* to the yellow *P. helodoxa* or the orange *P. bulleyana*. At the front of the house is a splendid herbaceous border which looks at its best in early summer.

The first garden you come to as you

enter the property is the walled garden on the left, laboriously constructed by Osgood Mackenzie with its typical Scottish mixture of vegetables, flowers, fruit and gnarled old apple trees. There is also a herbaceous border, planned to reach its peak in late June and early July, backed by climbers such as *Garrya elliptica* with its catkins, and the lovely *Clematis rehderiana* from China. There is also a collection of shrub and species roses, complemented by grey and silver plants. There are glasshouses open to the public, one containing a collection of Victorian-style conservatory plants, the other orchids and bromeliads. Bear left from the walled garden to the rock garden, at its best in spring and summer. It has some spectacular gentians in August, notably *Gentiana saxosa* and *G. septemfida*, and impressive silver-foliaged plants from New Zealand, celmisia and raoulia. 'Japan' comes next, named after a large Japanese cherry tree which no longer exists. The garden now has a tropical look with tree ferns and Chusan palms. Look for *Mitraria coccinea* from Chile, with seed capsules like bishops' mitres.

The famous woodland garden, however, dominates the little peninsula. A group of Scots and Corsican pines, among Osgood Mackenzie's first plantings, provide shelter for some spectacular shrubs. There is the *Rhododendron giganteum*, for instance, which was originally raised from seed sent home from Yunnan province of China by George Forrest, one of Scotland's greatest plant collectors. It is the largest of all known rhododendrons, reaching some 80 ft (24 m) in the wild. There are also peat banks and a pond,

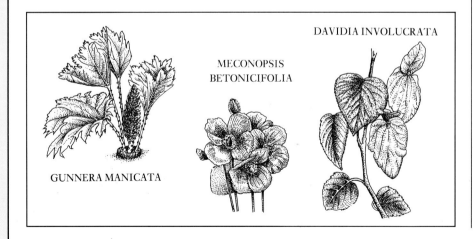

DAVIDIA INVOLUCRATA

MECONOPSIS
BETONICIFOLIA

GUNNERA MANICATA

housing a wealth of unusual plants, and a wet valley dominated by the large-leaved *Gunnera manicata* from Brazil, with leaves up to 6 ft (2 m) in width. Follow the curve of the peninsula to the rhododendron walk with its famous rhododendrons – the reason why most people come to Inverewe – but do not miss the strange umbrella

---

This fine garden was begun in 1862, and is now full of a wide range of magnificent plants

plant (*Peltiphyllum peltatum*) whose flowers appear in February, followed by leaves which look like open umbrellas. Nearby is the Peace Plot with many beautiful woodland flowers, including meconopsis, the dog's tooth violet (*Erythronium dens-canis*) and primulas. From here it is a short way to Bambooselem, where the *Magnolia campbellii* is situated. Look, too, for the climbing hydrangea (*Hydrangea petiolaris*) almost covering a tall larch, and the handkerchief tree (*Davidia involucrata*) with its tissue-like

white bracts. Finally you reach 'America', a drier sunnier area where there are two strange plants of the pineapple family: *Ochagavia lindleyana*, and *Fascicularia bicolor* with its bright red centre. There are also two unusual eucalyptuses: the silver *Eucalyptus coccifera* and the green *E. vernicosa*. In addition, there is a rare variegated turkey oak (*Quercus cerris* 'Variegata') that is worth seeing.

6 miles (9.5 km) north-east of Gairloch, on the A832 (map page 61)

Continued from page 109

walls and balustrades are generously clothed in climbers, especially wisteria, which winds its way around stone columns. And from the cloisters which Peto built to house some of the sculpture there are views of the countryside around.

2½ miles (4 km) south-west of
Bradford on Avon, off the A36
(map pages 58–9)

ISABELLA PLANTATION   LONDON

When standing in this cool, quiet, leafy woodland, it is difficult to imagine that you are so near to one of the busiest roads out of London. The plantation covers 42 acres (17 ha) in all, and was started in Victorian times in a rather desultory fashion. After World War II it was developed into what we see today by the guiding hand of J.W. Fisher. The plantation is best known for its splendid collection of rhododendrons and azaleas, growing together under a roof of mature deciduous trees, as they do at CLAREMONT (Surrey), further out of town. It also houses a large number of moisture-loving plants which can be found grouped together around the stream, and beside the ponds and the lake. May is the best time to visit this oasis in Richmond Park, when the plantation is in its full glory: the azaleas are out, the primulas in flower and the hostas at their best. Everywhere there are carpets of tiny wild flowers. Here, too, are spring bulbs, many of them species, and camellias add an exotic touch.

The plantation is criss-crossed with paths which take you through the woodland to the heather garden and the collection of willows below. Children love to visit the place, particularly enjoying the lake and the stepping stones across the stream. In winter it is the turn of the witch hazels to shine, and the dogwoods show off their coloured stems.

In Richmond Park, off the A307, A205
and A3 (map page 59)

JENKYN PLACE   HAMPSHIRE

Although you may not realize it at first sight, Jenkyn Place, set on the north side of the valley of the River Wey, is a relatively new garden, laid out and planted since the end of World War II over an area of 6 acres (2.4 ha), replacing what had largely been an Edwardian garden with gravel paths and formal beds. On the principle that a garden must not disclose all its secrets at first sight, the garden has been laid out as a series of rooms, in the SISSINGHURST CASTLE (Kent) tradition, planted so that there is something of interest to see all year round.

First you come to the Dutch garden with a fountain, flanked by farm buildings. On one side are some magnificent climbing roses – 'Madame Grégoire Staechelin', 'Madame Plantier', 'Gloire de Dijon', 'Albertine' and 'Lady Waterlow' to mention just a few – and other scented plants. The myrtle on the east wall was grown from a cutting from a bride's bouquet, and the four 18th-century lead tubs are filled with lemon-scented verbena. The sundial garden has mainly container plants, filled with a wide-ranging collection of pelargoniums in summer, many of them scented.

The rose garden combines both old-fashioned and

The sundial garden at Jenkyn Place

modern roses. The herbaceous borders are a delight in summer, and there are many ornaments in this pretty garden, placed with great care so that they add to, rather than detract from, the scenery. Finally, do not miss the whole range of magnolias, alpines and herbs.

North of Bentley, off the A31
(map page 59)

◆

KENSINGTON ROOF GARDEN   LONDON

This is by far the largest roof garden in Britain, $1\frac{1}{2}$ acres (0.6 ha) in extent, and it comes as a total surprise, situated in the heart of London. You forget that the huge variety of trees and shrubs are planted in soil only $2\frac{1}{2}$ ft (75 cm) deep, and that you are perched 100 ft (30 m) above the traffic and the shoppers below.

The gardens were built in 1938 by landscape architect Ralph Hancock, an ambitious scheme to provide an extra attraction on top of a department store. The building had to be reinforced to take the weight of the soil, and wells had to be bored in the street below to bring water up for the plants. Chinese moon windows were built into the surrounding walls so that shoppers could look out over the rooftops of London.

Over 5000 different plants grow here, not simply the shallow-rooting azaleas, and roses in profusion, but conifers, hawthorns and laburnums. There is also a paperbark maple, a willow and a catalpa. The main feature is probably the Spanish garden with its avenue of fan palms, while vines, peaches and figs add to the tropical feel. Then, in contrast, there is a quiet Tudor garden with formal beds, and around the edges of it all an English woodland garden with a small lake by which a flock of flamingoes is usually found.

In the centre of London, at 99
Kensington High Street, with entry
from Derry Street (map page 59)

◆

The newly-restored Palm House at Kew

KEW: ROYAL BOTANIC GARDENS   LONDON

Now known by Londoners as a pleasant place for an outing, Kew grew from two estates belonging to the royal family. The gardens themselves were started in the 1700s by Queen Augusta, mother of George III, on 9 acres (3.6 ha) of ground. It was then that the orangery, pagoda, ruined arch and many other features were built. The grounds were eventually handed over to the nation by Queen Victoria.

Today the gardens cover 300 acres (120 ha) in all, and despite popular belief that they are a public park, their real purpose is to serve a scientific institution which identifies plants from all over the world and breeds them for distribution. In this way, Kew plays a vital role on the conservation front. It also houses a school of horticulture, a herbarium, and one of the best botanical libraries in the world.

The gardens contain many collections of plants grouped together. Around 2000 species of annuals and perennials can be found in the walled herbaceous ground; there is a rose garden, a grass garden and a bamboo garden. The rock garden, laid out in 1882, is at its best in spring, when the bulbs and many mountain flowers come into bloom. This is the time to visit the 'mound' and the woodland garden with its wild flowers. In autumn the heather garden is at its best.

The Duchess's Border has some interesting plants from far-flung places such as New Zealand and Chile. The Queen's Garden is a superb reconstruction of a 17th-century garden with parterres, pleached alleys, and herbs and other plants that were commonplace in our gardens 300 years ago, all carefully labelled to show how they were used. Kew has a vast collection of trees and shrubs, among them some fine camellias and lilacs. Finally, do not forget to visit the glasshouses, with the newly-restored Palm House as Kew's crowning glory.

South of Kew Bridge, off the A307
(map page 59)

◆

KIFTSGATE COURT GARDEN   GLOUCESTERSHIRE

The garden of this 19th-century house with its Georgian façade was mainly created by Mrs Muir, grandmother of the present owner, in the years after World War I, helped by her neighbour, Major Johnston of HIDCOTE MANOR (Gloucestershire). She transformed what was basically a formal paved garden and a field with steep wooded banks on the edge of the Cotswolds into a dramatic and very personal garden. Here she created Kiftsgate's yellow border,

Kiftsgate Court Garden, created after World War I

a wide band of yellow flowers, ranging from sulphur to deep gold, offset by blue and purple and backed by mahogany-coloured foliage, and the famous rose border – a grass path is edged on both sides by a hedge of *Rosa gallica* 'Versicolor'. Some of the plants have reverted to one of their original parents, the Apothecary's rose, giving a bizarre effect when they are in flower. But the main feature is the famous *Rosa filipes* 'Kiftsgate', a rampant climber which takes up more than half the space on the left-hand side. Many people come away from Kiftsgate's garden shop with a specimen of this vigorous plant, little realizing its strength, for it is said that if ever Kiftsgate fell into decay, the rose would seize its chance and become the ramparts of a Sleeping Beauty palace all by itself. It is a remarkable sight when in flower during mid July, covered with panicles of white blooms, cascading down in great white showers. However, there are many more roses – old-fashioned, modern and species – *Rosa soulieana*, for instance, with its beautiful grey foliage, which can be found on the side of the white sunk garden, and *Rosa sericea* 'Heather Muir', named after the garden's creator. In addition, there are many other unusual plants and shrubs.

4 miles (6.5 km) north-east of Chipping
Camden, off the B4081 (map page 59)

KNIGHTSHAYES COURT   DEVON

This is one of the finest gardens in Devon, 40 acres (16 ha) of fine specimen trees, rare shrubs and a splendid display of bulbs in spring. Originally laid out formally by Edward Kemp, a pupil of Joseph Paxton, in Victorian times, it was later considered too labour-intensive (500 pots of chrysanthemums, alone, were used along the south front). Sir John and Lady Amory replanned it in the 1950s, scaling down the formal beds, putting in more permanent shrubs and herbaceous plants, and training climbers like the magnificent climbing roses against the house. The park has fine trees, particularly evergreens such as the cedar of Lebanon and Douglas fir, and there is also a willow garden – another innovation of the Heathcoat-Amorys. One of Knightshayes' great features is the delightful woodland garden with magnolias, rhododendrons and azaleas underplanted with hellebores, anemones and, in other places, bulbs such as grape hyacinths, fritillaries and cyclamen. To the east of the house, among Kemp's castellated yew hedges, is a pretty paved garden featuring pink and silver flowers, with standard wisterias and two stone benches which came from the old Bank of England (demolished in 1933). Another larger enclosed garden, once a bowling green, houses a lily pond inhabited by golden orfe. South of these gardens is Knightshayes' famous topiary fox and hounds careering over hedges, and first pruned in this shape in the 1920s.

2 miles (3 km) north of Tiverton, east
of the A396 (map page 58)

KNOLE   KENT

Knole is surrounded by walled gardens which were completed at the end of the 16th century. The house itself, which sits in one corner of the gardens, dates from 1456, and was where Vita Sackville-West spent her childhood. She had her own garden there but, as she says in her book *Gardens and Gardeners*, 'weeds grow too fast and flowers too slowly'. She let it get untidy, the gardeners would descend and tidy it up, so she felt it was not really her garden at all. The gardens at Knole were laid out formally by Thomas Akres in 1710, and much of his design, as far as paths and divisions between beds are concerned, has survived to the present day; the Sackvilles were loathe to change the design, even though 'Capability' Brown's new landscape movement threatened.

On two sides of the house are lawns with terraced slopes. There is an old-fashioned herb garden, an orchard, and a splendid display of rhododendrons and azaleas, with a huge old wisteria growing along one wall. In one corner of the gardens is the wilderness, the 18th-century precursor of the Victorian shrubbery, with some fine old trees including limes. Flags and large ferns decorate the bog garden. The present owners are restoring other parts of the garden to their former splendour. Surrounding the property is a beautiful park containing fallow and Japanese deer.

At the south-east end of Sevenoaks,
just east of the A225 (map page 59)

LEONARDSLEE   WEST SUSSEX

Leonardslee is a large and spectacular woodland garden in a magnificent setting, a wooded valley extending to some 80 acres (32 ha), laced by streams which have been dammed to form a series of lakes. This is the place to see what is probably the finest collection of rhododendrons, azaleas, camellias and magnolias in Britain, backed by old oaks, beeches, birches and conifers. Centuries of leafmould have created an acid soil ideal for all ericaceous plants, but it is the rhododendrons and azaleas that take the centre

stage. Being on a slope, and shaded, the garden seldom dries out, hence the luxurious vegetation. And of particular interest to the small-space gardener are the dwarf azaleas and rhododendrons that cover the huge rockery.

Sir Edmund Loder, who came to the garden in 1889, was responsible for creating the landscape that visitors see today. Interested in all forms of nature, he not only introduced many exotic plants to Leonardslee but the wallabies as well, whose descendants can be seen hopping around part of the garden. There is a camellia walk and grove, but the dell with its fine rhododendron hybrids is surely one of the loveliest parts of the garden. There is a richness and variety of trees at Leonardslee: a deodar in the dell has the oldest rhododendron in the garden, dating from the early 19th century, underneath it, and there is a fine tulip tree (*Liriodendron tulipifera*) by the middle walk. Look also for the handkerchief tree (*Davidia involucrata*) with its white bracts in May, and *Acer palmatum* 'Senkaki', the coral bark maple, as well as a rare form of the Chusan palm (*Trachycarpus fortunei* var. surculosa) which forms clumps. The storms that caused such havoc in the south of England actually did Leonardslee some good, according to one of Sir Edmund's descendants, Captain Loder. It got rid of a lot of old and ailing trees and let in more sunlight, enabling half as much garden again to be opened to the public. A permanent exhibition of bonsai trees has recently been set up.

5 miles (8 km) south-east of Horsham,
on the A281 (map page 59)

LONGLEAT   WILTSHIRE

'Capability' Brown and Humphry Repton, who both had a hand in creating the landscape at Longleat, would be surprised today to find lions and zebras strolling through the safari park that much of the land has become. But 'Capability' Brown's vista, a series of lakes and groups of trees, can still be seen in some of its original glory, viewed from

Left *A view down the valley at Leonardslee*

'Heaven's Gate' to the south-east of the house which stands on a site that the present Marquess of Bath's ancestor, John Thynne, bought for £53 in 1540. There are other things to see, too, including a wisteria-clad orangery built in 1802, heavy with the scent of lemon verbena and containing many interesting tender plants. Behind it lies a secret garden with old-fashioned shrub roses, petulant peacocks strutting about, and a bizarre statue of Sir Jeffrey Hudson, an aristocratic dwarf who is said to have been served up in a pie at court in the time of Charles I. The avenue of pleached limes and a knot garden were designed by Russell Page who made numerous improvements to the general layout. There is a wide herbaceous border, much clipped box, and splendid lawns. There are fairground attractions at Longleat, but another attraction of a more natural kind is what is believed to be the world's largest maze, making the one at HAMPTON COURT PALACE (London) look like a toy. It is laid out in curves rather than right angles, and although it was planted as recently as 1978, its 2 miles or more (over 3 km) of hedges are now high enough for you to become properly lost. There is also a rather touching animal cemetery with graves of pets belonging to the Bath family and their friends.

4 miles (6.5 km) south of Frome, off the
A362 (map pages 58–9)

LUTON HOO   BEDFORDSHIRE

This is a 'Capability' Brown landscape, with clusters of fine old trees, most of which were actually planted in Victorian times, after Brown's death. The cedars and oaks stand out particularly. Brown also created the lake out of the River Lea by widening its banks. On the south front of the vast Robert Adam house are balustraded terraces designed by William Henry Romaine-Walker. Here, a formal garden is crowned by two huge magnolias, and a large herbaceous border has recently been restored. Below, lies an Edwardian rose garden with more than 3000 large-flowered and standard roses, set in eight large beds edged with clipped box and backed by yew hedges and topiary.

Continued on page 121

Guided Tour

LEVENS HALL   CUMBRIA

People have been coming to see the unique topiary garden at Levens Hall since the 1700s, when the journey even from Kendal was an arduous one, due to the terrible state of the roads. It is known the world over as one of the best examples of its kind, set off by the splendid stone house, which dates in part from *c.* 1250, and has been in the hands of the same family for over 700 years.

Levens Hall's topiary was planted for a Colonel Grahme in 1692 by a fashionable expert of that time, a Monsieur Guillaume Beaumont, gardener to James II. Three hundred years later they remain intact, the only example of his work still to be seen today. Part of the reason for its survival is that Colonel Grahme's daughter stubbornly refused to bow to the 18th-century fashion for 'natural' landscape, and kept the intricate parterres and topiary when they were being swept away elsewhere.

The gardens lie to the left of the house as you approach it, and the green of the topiary figures ranges from near gold to near black, depending on the shrubs from which they are cut, which gives them an almost unreal appearance. In the centre of the garden are the chess pieces, precisely set in neat beds. Other topiary shapes have names like wigwam, umbrella, Dutch oven and judge's wig; in addition there are the more conventional spirals, pyramids and globes, and a parterre in the corner too. Still more yew is clipped to resemble the battlements of a castle. The topiary looks beautiful in the snow, when it takes on a lighter, more ghostly effect.

New pieces were added in Victorian times – you can spot them easily because they are cut from golden rather than dark green yew. The overall solidity of the topiary is offset by pretty plantings of annual flowers and roses which add welcome colour in summer. And the vivid flame flower (*Tropaeolum speciosum*) rambles over some of the high hedges, adding a splash of scarlet here and there.

Things have to be replaced from time to time – at one stage 9 miles (14.5 km) of box edging had to be replanted, but the garden goes on very much as it did in Beaumont's day, though he could never have envisaged the height his chess pieces would reach. It takes four gardeners to keep up the colourful displays of bedding in the parterres in spring and autumn, when more than 15,000 plants are used. The huge beech hedges are clipped in September, using trestles 15 ft (4.5 m) high. Shaping the topiary goes on through the winter, and sometimes yields surprises: at the turn of the century a gardener found a toby jug, probably from

Examples of topiary shapes to be seen at Levens Hall

the 1700s, embedded in the branches of one of the trees.

Do not miss the rest of the garden when you go to Levens Hall. Behind the house are handsome avenues of tall thick

The remarkable topiary garden, first planted in 1692, is one of the best examples in the world

beech hedges which divide the area in quarters and lead to a circle of immaculate turf in the centre. There is also a bowling green where at one time annual parties were held in May, when the locals came to feast on the radishes. In addition, there is a little herb garden, some colourful spring beds and borders, and one of the earliest known ha-has, dividing the garden from the parkland surrounding it.

Levens Hall also has a splendid park with goats and black fallow deer, described in 1790 by West in his *Guide to the Lakes* as 'the sweetest spot that Fancy can imagine'. The 20th century has intervened, however, and you now have to cross a busy road to visit it.

5 miles (8 km) south of Kendal, on the A6 (map page 60)

Continued from page 117

The rock garden, hidden in a dip, was a present from Lord Wernher to his wife at the beginning of the century. Small pools with water-lilies run through the centre. Stand on the bridge over the main pool to get the best view of the newly-restored scree beds which feature little *Iris reticulata*, sedums, thymes, with heathers and other ericaceous plants growing in the peat walls. The dwarf conifers remain from the original planting, as do some of the maples.

2 miles (3 km) south-east of Luton, off
the A1081 (map page 59)

◆

MELBOURNE HALL   DERBYSHIRE

Here you have an almost perfect early 18th-century garden, one of the finest in the country, as it has remained virtually unchanged since it was designed by Thomas Coke, helped by his sister Betsy who was in charge while he was in London. It is a combination of the formal and the informal, with numerous classical statues, pools fed by natural springs and crowned with fountains, and vistas designed to lead the eye to one point of interest after another. Heavily influenced by the style of Le Nôtre but covering just 16 acres (6.4 ha), it is much smaller in scale than classic French gardens of that time.

The gardens, first laid out by Sir John Coke at the beginning of the 17th century, are divided into four main parts. The banked-up terrace extending along the eastern front is the principal one, with formal lawns stepped down to a lake. Then there is a forecourt, a walled garden behind the house, and the orchard and the kitchen garden. Sir John's grandson, Colonel Coke, married the wealthy Mary Leventhorpe who brought enough money into the family to pay for some extensive alterations to the original design. But the garden we see today is largely the work of Thomas, who inherited the property in 1696.

Entering the garden via the courtyard, go down the library walk, and as you turn through the yew hedge on

Left *The fine rose garden at Luton Hoo*

The yew tunnel at Melbourne Hall

your right you will catch your first glimpse of the east façade of the house. Turn left and follow the gravel path down to the Great Basin, as the pool was once known, and you will come to the Birdcage, an intricately wrought arbour of ironwork made by the famous 18th-century smith Robert Bakewell, whose foundry was nearby. To the left of the basin is the famous ancient yew tunnel made from trees that were originally trained over a wooden framework but which now arch high overhead of their own accord, making a tunnel of twisted trunks. The gardens are also known for their classical statues of mythological figures, cupids and kneeling slaves, some of them by Jan van Nost.

8 miles (13 km) south of Derby, on the
A514 (map page 59)

◆

MYDDELTON HOUSE LONDON

The 4 acres (1.6 ha) of garden at Myddelton House were largely the creation of the famous gardener and writer Edward A. Bowles (1865-1954). He was an enthusiastic plant collector who had a profound effect on the gardening public of his time. In 1889 he brought his first plants back from abroad after a holiday in Italy and set about turning the dull family garden, complete with Victorian shrubbery, into the magical place it is today. After Bowles' death the garden became overgrown, but the Lee Valley Regional Park Authority have now restored it to its former splendour.

Despite past neglect, the garden, famous for its diverse collection of plants, seems to have an intensely personal feel about it, as if Bowles were still alive. The plants are an eclectic mixture – there is an area which he dubbed 'the Lunatic Asylum', with a collection of unusual and bizarre plants, mostly dwarf and twisted forms of common shrubs and flowers, such as a twisted hawthorn, an oak-leaved laburnum, and the distinctive corkscrew hazel.

A spectacular National Collection of Irises is housed here, with some very unusual forms of this elegant flower. In spring the garden is a riot of colour as millions of bulbs bloom. Woodpeckers, treecreepers and other birds make a visit worthwhile for the naturalist, too. The autumn crocuses and late-flowering irises are a delight in the autumn, as are the nerines, the splendid pink South African lilies which flower into November. When Edward Bowles died, his ashes were scattered over the rock garden which he had created with the help of his friend, the alpine specialist Reginald Farrer.

*At Bull's Cross, north of Enfield, at
junction 25 of the M25 (map page 59)*

———◆———

NYMANS GARDEN WEST SUSSEX

In 1890 Ludwig Messel, encouraged by his friends, decided to design the garden around his newly-acquired house at Handcross. The friends happened to be gardening pundits Gertrude Jekyll and William Robinson, so it is not surprising that the result is a fascinating 30-acre (12 ha) mixture of formality and informality. First the walled garden was made, with its herbaceous borders (Robinson had a hand in these) and topiary, then the sunk garden with its collection of flowering shrubs and bedding plants. About the same time the pinetum, a dense band of conifers, was planted, which still has some rare old trees today. Then Messel added an avenue of limes along the eastern boundary and a Japanese garden.

Other members of the family took over, developing the gardens to their present-day splendour. One planted a collection of magnolias, another made a rose garden. Ludwig Messel's grand-daughter brought back camellia cuttings from Portugal which have grown into sizeable shrubs. A rock garden and a heather garden both have a period look about them, and, in true turn-of-the-century tradition, there is a wild garden and rhododendron wood – Nymans, incidentally, is not far from LEONARDSLEE (West Sussex).

Nymans House itself was all but destroyed by fire in 1947, but the ruins have been left standing, forming a modern folly, a foil for some spectacular climbers and a screen for tender plants.

*South of Handcross village, east of the
A23 (map page 59)*

———◆———

PACKWOOD HOUSE WARWICKSHIRE

An element of mystery hangs over this garden – what, exactly, are the strange topiary shapes in it supposed to be? It is said by some that the trees represent the Sermon on the Mount, with Christ and his Apostles at one end and the audience at the other – though the 'multitude' to whom the sermon is being preached are in fact relatively recent additions to the garden and not part of the original plan (which is known to have been in existence in the 1750s). Now grown to immense proportions (they have to be clipped by men on hydraulic lifts), they certainly give a brooding, almost sinister, air to the relatively small area in which they are placed.

The dovecote at Nymans Garden, seen through clipped yew hedges

Apart from the topiary, there is much to be seen at Packwood. There is a very attractive sunken garden, edged with yew, which features some imaginatively planted herbaceous borders with herbs mixed in with the flowers. This is a very domestic garden, attached to a beautiful Tudor house, with all kinds of fascinating detail. There is an interesting plunge pool, for instance, hidden away behind yew hedges and dating from the 17th century. One of the attractive gazebos contains a fireplace: here fires were lit to warm the wall behind and help ripen the fruit growing against it. Outside the walled gardens, parkland merges into the countryside, with an attractive lake.

**2 miles (3 km) east of Hockley Heath,
off the A34 (map page 59)**

◆

PAINSHILL PARK   SURREY

At the end of the 18th century Painshill was one of the finest and most fashionable landscape gardens in Britain, if not in Europe. The Hon. Charles Hamilton, a gifted and imaginative designer and plantsman, created it from 250 acres (100 ha) of barren heathland, with a 14-acre (5.6 ha) lake as its centrepiece. Known now as a 'jewel in the nation's heritage crown', it is difficult to realize today that the garden suffered from the most appalling neglect in recent years and was only rescued from total extinction at the eleventh hour. After years in private ownership, Painshill had fallen into the hands of developers and much of the land had been sold off; it was only the efforts of a determined local pressure group that stopped the garden from disappearing altogether. Much of the restoration work was, remarkably, carried out through Manpower Services Commission schemes under which the young unemployed were given training and taught skills.

Today, a leisurely circuit walk will bring you to the Gothic temple, the water wheel, and a Gothic folly built as a ruined abbey. There is an island to visit on the lake,

Left *The sunken garden at Packwood House*

and breathtaking vistas at every turn, just as Hamilton intended. Most of the restoration work has been of buildings rather than planting, but there is also a field of bluebells (*Hyacinthoides non-scripta*), for instance, and more than 300 new trees have been planted. Some landscaping has been done behind the Gothic temple, ringing the site of an amphitheatre with trees and shrubs, and in a trial bed are species that Hamilton is believed to have planted. There is talk, too, of replanting the original vineyard from which Hamilton used to make his own champagne. Flowers or no flowers, it is a remarkable place to visit, if only to see the pencil cedar (*Juniperus viginiana*) planted before 1770 in the Gothic temple meadow. It is now about 60 ft (18 m) tall, and has a mountain ash seedling (*Sorbus aucuparia*) growing in its cleft.

**1 mile (1.5 km) west of Cobham, on the
A245 (map page 59)**

◆

PARNHAM HOUSE   DORSET

This enchanting Tudor manor house is now the home of John Makepeace, the furniture designer, and the splendid 14-acre (5.6 ha) garden shows just what can be achieved even on an exposed site that is prone to frost – a task that falls to Mrs Makepeace. When they took over the house in 1976, she faced a series of walkways and courtyards, an 80-yard (73 m) long Italian garden and woodland, all of which had been neglected, plus 8 acres (3.2 ha) of lawns to mow. She set to work, replacing labour-intensive bedding plants with something more permanent, making herbaceous borders, clearing a dense wilderness, and bringing the estate up to the impressive standard that it shows today.

There is much to see: the Ladies' Terrace against the south front, balustraded and decorated with twin gazebos, makes an ideal spot from which to view the topiary of 50 yews, clipped in pyramid shapes and separated by rills, little channels of spring water. Just beyond the bridge is an iris garden. Two ginkgo trees, examples of an ancient type of

Parnham House's gardens have recently been restored

conifer known to have existed for 160 million years, stand guard on the bank nearby. There are roses everywhere. The front court is overflowing with roses such as 'Albertine', while hybrid musks such as 'Pax', 'Penelope' and 'Buff Beauty' fill the borders, underplanted in places with *Ajuga reptans* 'Burgundy Glow' (a purple-leaved version of wild bugle) and *Persicaria affinis* 'Darjeeling Red'. The austere lines of the original Italian garden are now softened by two splendid herbaceous borders. One of them is backed by the high wall of the former kitchen garden, which has small fire-places set in the curved end, once used to heat a complex system of flues within the wall to protect fruit trees on the other side. The old kitchen garden itself, which covers 4 acres (1.6 ha), now contains fruit trees and wild flowers. The yew hedges lead on the other side to an area of woodland featuring palms and bamboos, where outsize statues of Morecambe and Wise lurk among the rhododendrons. The days when the head gardener wore a top hat and white gloves

at Parnham have long since gone. The 18 men employed at the turn of the century have been replaced now by just two, under the enthusiastic direction and supervision of Jennie Makepeace.

To the south of Beaminster, on the
A3066 (map pages 58–9)

◆

PENRHYN CASTLE   GWYNEDD

Like Arundel Castle in West Sussex, Penrhyn is a Victorian fake, built in neo-Norman style, complete with gatehouse, on a superb site. It has with it a Victorian walled garden which, taking advantage of the mild moist climate, houses a collection of tender plants that could not be expected to flourish elsewhere. There are a number of Chilean plants, the fire bush for example, and tall eucryphias, also natives of South America, which seem to have taken to their surroundings, producing quantities of beautiful white flowers in August.

The garden is terraced, making the most of ground that slopes away from the castle. The top terrace, in typical country-house style, is a formal one with box parterres, lily ponds and a loggia. Tender plants make their appearance again in the form of climbers clinging to the castle walls. There is a handkerchief tree (*Davidia involucrata*), with its pocket-handkerchief-like bracts appearing in May. There is also a Japanese cornus, with its strawberry-like fruits and leaves that turn bright crimson in the autumn.

The lower terrace has a pretty pergola covered in scented honeysuckle, and there is a tranquil water garden, too, highlighted by a large *Gunnera manicata*. There is a wild garden, while rhododendrons, azaleas and camellias clothe the rest of the castle slopes, making a perfect flower picture in late spring.

3 miles (5 km) east of Bangor, on the
A5122 (map page 60)

◆

PENSHURST PLACE   KENT

The garden at Penshurst is over 600 years old – the age of the original house – making it one of the oldest gardens in private ownership in Britain. Over the years many people have had a hand in its design. The first was Sir Philip Sidney, who shifted an entire slope, moving thousands of tons of soil to create a level site for the huge formal garden. The most notable was the 2nd Lord De L'Isle in Victorian times, who revived Penshurst after years of neglect, restoring the 17th-century layout. The Italian garden, as this formal area is now called, dominates the scene with its four panelled parterres of planting, divided by gravel paths; from the Tudor terrace the effect is softened by the estate woodlands beyond.

Penshurst is actually a series of separate gardens, each enclosure contrasting with its neighbour and concentrating on particular plants. There is a magnolia garden, for instance, designed by John Codrington, a rose garden with floribundas – imaginatively hedged with *Berberis thunbergii* 'Atropurpurea Nana' – rue, and standard roses towering over a carpet of silvery lambs' ears (*Stachys byzantina*). The splendid double border under arched apple trees was planted to the design of the late Lanning Roper, and there is a border, more than 100 yards (90 m) long, of massed peonies which flower in late May. Penshurst offers a succession of colourful displays from spring to early autumn.

The Italian garden at Penshurst Place

In June and July the parterre is aflame with red roses framed in box, and the wide herbaceous borders offer a display of spectacular flowers throughout the summer. There is a nut garden, a theatre garden, even a union flag garden, planted in red, white and blue, and Diana's Bath – a lily pond scented with water hyacinths (*Aponogeton*) which flower from spring to autumn. 'We went to Penshurst famous for its gardens and excellent fruit,' wrote John Evelyn in 1652. The fruit is still there in the form of an apple orchard full of Bramleys. There is even a political planting: an attractive avenue of limes installed in the 18th century to signify a family sympathy with the Whig cause.

North-west of Tunbridge Wells, off the A2176 (map page 59)

◆

PITMEDDEN GARDEN   GRAMPIAN

The Great Garden at Pitmedden is one of the few surviving 17th-century gardens in Britain. It was originally created by Sir Alexander Seton, later to become Lord Pitmedden, who landscaped the steeply sloping ground to the east of the house to make a terrace from which to view the parterre below. At either end are pavilions with ogival roofs, very similar to those at Kinross in Tayside. The gardens, however, fell into disrepair and by the beginning of the 19th century the priceless parterres were being used to house fruit and vegetables.

When the National Trust for Scotland took it over in 1952, the patterns had all but disappeared and restoration was hampered by the fact that all the original garden plans and pictures had been destroyed by fire. So the garden was re-created using the designs for a similar parterre at Holyrood House in Edinburgh. As a tribute to Sir Alexander, there is a section laid out in the shape of a Scottish thistle and saltire, and a square with his coat of arms, motto and the date 1675. Three miles (5 km) of box edging were used to get the parterre to its present state of perfection, and 40,000 plants. A fountain was added to the centre of the garden, made from pieces of stone taken from

The box-edged parterres at Pitmedden Garden

the castle surroundings and from the Cross Fountain at Linlithgow in Lothian. There is also a herb garden, and fine herbaceous borders, but it is the parterres that take centre stage here.

1 mile (1.5 km) west of Pitmedden
village, on the A920 (map page 61)

◆

PLAS NEWYDD GWYNEDD

Nestling on the bank of the Menai Strait, this elegant 18th-century house, with its mural by Rex Whistler, is surrounded by a fine spring and summer garden which is at its peak in May and June when the rhododendrons are in flower. Designed originally by Humphry Repton, it is a living lesson in the history of horticulture. And the setting could not be more superb – grounds sloping down to the spectacular Menai Strait, with Snowdonia in the background. After Repton's original planting, of which many oaks, beeches and sycamores remain, the main alterations to the gardens were made by the 6th Marquess of Anglesey in the 1930s. He planted a great number of rare Himalayan rhododendrons – follow 'Lady Uxbridge's Walk' to find them – as well as blue cedars, ginkgos and tulip trees, and groups of azaleas, magnolias and maples. The Marquess was also responsible for the formal Italianate garden with its yew hedges and Mediterranean cypresses. Built on two terraces to the south of the house, the original planting of roses has now been softened by the addition of shrubs and herbaceous plants.

The gardens fell into neglect during World War II, but the present Marquess has revitalized them, adding in particular to the collection of rhododendrons which thrive in the mild humid air. The best time to go to Plas Newydd is in the spring when the camellias and rhododendrons are in bloom, and a spectacular show of white flowers on the *Viburnum tomentosum* makes a perfect foil for the reds and the pinks.

Situated on Anglesey, to the south of
the Menai Bridge, on the B4080
(map page 60)

◆

POLESDEN LACEY SURREY

This garden of 17 acres (7 ha) in a splendid setting on the North Downs has a long history attached to it. The poet Richard Brinsley Sheridan worked on the garden here, making the long terraced walk, but the house in which he lived has gone. The present 19th-century mansion became the setting for a series of glittering country house parties from Edwardian times onwards, when the Hon. Mrs Ronnie Greville lived and entertained here – the present Queen Mother was one of her guests and there is still a very nostalgic feel about the place. The gardens came into the hands of the National Trust in 1944.

A great deal of planting was done in Victorian times;

Continued on page 132

Looking through a circular portal in the wall at Polesden Lacey, to the armillary sphere sundial

Guided Tour

◆

POWIS CASTLE   POWYS

The gardens of Powis Castle, with their famous hanging terraces, are the greatest surviving example in Britain of the Italianate Baroque garden. And although their severe design and regimented planting must have looked strange at first against the craggy irregular shape of the castle, time and maturing trees have softened their lines so that they now seem almost to blend with each other.

They are believed to have been masterminded by the architect William Winde, who worked on the 1st Marquess of Powis' London house in the late 1680s. But others were also involved, notably Adrian Duval, a Frenchman, who probably designed the water gardens at the foot of the terraces, later turned into a lawn.

But the person who really explored the planting possibilities of these gardens, set as they are on a south-east-facing slope, was Violet, wife of the 4th Earl. In 1911 she began to replant and improve the terraces, work that has been continued since the 1950s by the National Trust.

There are, in effect, two distinct types of garden at Powis. The terraces are made from limestone so only lime-tolerant plants can grow there. In contrast, the wilderness on the other side of the valley is formed on acid soil, allowing a wide range of rhododendrons, azaleas and other acid-loving plants to thrive.

You enter the gardens to the right of the top terrace, which has some fine 18th-century topiary pieces and, among them, borders of trees, plants and shrubs, some of them tender, which give a subtropical effect – the palm-like *Cordyline australis*, for instance, and New Zealand flax (*Phormium tenax*) with its sword-like leaves. Past the big yew tree, you come to the rose borders and, at the back, a hedge of a white form of fuchsia, the South American *Fuchsia magellanica* 'Alba'. Many roses are trained against the wall, notably *Rosa wichuraiana*, parent of many modern ramblers, *R. soulieana* from China, and the Himalayan musk rose, *R. brunonii*. At the end of the terrace is an ancient yew hedge over 30 ft (9 m) high and 12 ft (3.5 m) wide.

The second, or aviary, terrace is given over to plants that enjoy dry sunny conditions: helichrysums, for example, with plantings in bright colours on the eastern side and softer pastels on the western end. Here ceanothus and cistus make an attractive show, while the former aviary houses a collection of tender fragrant rhododendrons, most of them from the Himalayas. Below, on the main terrace, is the orangery. Once heated for overwintering citrus trees in tubs, it now houses a range of tough plants that can tolerate very little light and no heating. On either side the

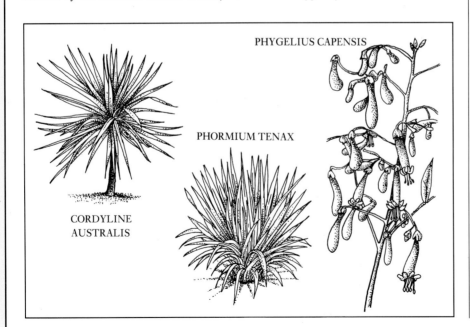

PHYGELIUS CAPENSIS

PHORMIUM TENAX

CORDYLINE
AUSTRALIS

box-edged mixed borders are designed to give their most spectacular display in midsummer. Here you will find climbers such as *Clematis flammula*, *C. tangutica* and the little-known indigofera, with its ferny foliage and pea-like purple-pink flowers. These are allowed to cascade down on to the apple slope terraces below. The western slope has a splendid autumn border, a mixture of herbaceous plants and shrubs. Here you will find Japanese maples, dogwoods with their coloured stems, spindles and more clematis (*C. jouiniana* and *C.* 'Lady Betty Balfour'). On the eastern side, a collection of hostas acts as ground cover to a variety of wall shrubs and climbers, the Cape figwort (*Phygelius capensis*) for instance, which is so colourful in summer. Look out, too, for a rare shrubby member of the violet family from New Zealand, *Hymenanthera crassifolia*. This border is at its best in May and June.

Cross the great lawn, and on the eastern side of the estate is the formal garden, approached via the box walk. At the turn of the century the Countess of Powis replaced the kitchen garden, which was all too visible from the castle, with a formal flower garden. The pyramid fruit trees were retained, however, but are underplanted with decorative ground-cover plants and dwarf bulbs. The south- and west-facing borders contain roses, and on the steep banks there are some flowering trees and shrubs, notably magnolias, mock oranges, aralias and

Statuary on the terrace at Powis, together with wisteria and white roses

laburnums. The formal garden leads to the croquet lawn with its spectacular long border of plants in cool colours, the blues of delphiniums and ceanothus followed by lavateras and many herbaceous flowers.

Finally, on the western side of the slopes there is the wilderness, a woodland garden on acid soil developed by William Emes. The lower walk leads to the Ladies' Bath past mixed species and

hybrid rhododendrons, hydrangeas and magnolias, with dramatic views of the castle. The Ladies' Bath, a Victorian bathing pool, is surrounded by ferns, and overlooked by the holly *Ilex × altaclerensis* 'Golden King', Young's weeping birch and winter cherry.

1 mile (1.5 km) south-west of Welshpool, off the A483 (map page 58)

Continued from page 128

20,000 trees were put in, and a walled garden that was probably used to grow vegetables. Now it is an Edwardian rose garden, laid out for Mrs Greville, where both modern and old-fashioned shrub roses intermingle with lavender and clematis. And over the pergolas you will find 'American Pillar' and 'Dorothy Perkins' roses. More lavender appears elsewhere in the garden, including some white varieties; there are herbaceous borders lavishly planted with luxurious flowers such as lilies and peonies, and also a rock garden built of limestone from the old county of Westmorland (now part of Cumbria).

Polesden Lacey is magical in the duller months of the year, too, when the mahonia and daphne come into their own in the winter garden. Sheridan's Long Walk has had to be replanted as the original trees became diseased and died, but the statues and garden ornaments that Mrs Greville installed still remain. So does she, for she is buried in a small enclosure to the west of the house, her tomb guarded, appropriately, by elegant French statues of the Four Seasons.

3 miles (5 km) north-west of Dorking,
off the A246 (map page 59)

◆

THE PRIORY   HEREFORD AND WORCESTER

The owners of The Priory, Mr and the Hon. Mrs Peter Healing, have created a magical garden since they took over the Georgian house and 4 acres (1.6 ha) at the beginning of World War II. The herbaceous borders here are quite outstanding. There are three in all, each very different from the other. One is almost completely red, with flowers ranging from scarlet to deep crimson and foliage from bronze to purple, offset perfectly by the sombre dark green of yew and the stone of the ruined priory. Facing the west side of the house is a many-coloured border with shrubs, herbaceous plants and annuals all playing their part, and the third massive border – 150 ft (45 m) long and 19 ft (6 m) deep – goes from cool to warm, graded from grey, silver and white, then yellow, warming up to red again.

There is a huge yew tree, thought to date from the 17th century and clipped into the shape of a giant bun. There is also a sunken garden with hydrangeas, hostas, lilies and peonies, a small arboretum and a secret early-summer garden, linked to the house by a pergola over which scramble climbing roses, clematis and vines. At its best in June, this small plot, enclosed by yew hedges and trees, contrasts with the more strident colours outside and is in pastel pinks, mauves and silver. At the far end of the pergola is a stream lined with water-loving plants, primulas, arums and a huge *Gunnera manicata*. The Priory is, as you can see, a series of enclosed spaces, with surprises round every corner.

In the village of Kemerton, 5 miles
(8 km) north-east of Tewkesbury, off
the B4080 (map pages 58–9)

◆

ROSEMOOR GARDEN   DEVON

An attack of the measles was the rather bizarre reason for the creation of the lovely gardens at Rosemoor, set in the valley of the River Torridge. Lady Anne Palmer, who owned the 40-acre (16 ha) property at the time, went to Spain to recuperate from the measles, met garden designer Collingwood Ingram there, and visited his garden in England on her return. This inspired her to start an 8-acre (3.2 ha) garden of her own at Rosemoor, which has grown over the years to be a plantsman's paradise. Travelling all over the world, Lady Anne brought back plants from places as diverse as Papua New Guinea, Japan and South America, and they thrive in their new setting in this mild, moist microclimate.

Rosemoor is now owned by the Royal Horticultural Society which has established it as their first regional centre and garden, and plans to increase its acreage of planting and provide demonstration beds, together with many other facilities which will turn it into WISLEY (Surrey) in miniature in the west of England. It already houses more than 4000 different plants including, unexpectedly among all this exotica, collections of hollies and dogwoods. The

Society has now planted over 1000 yews and 2000 roses in the square field, their new development area. The woodland plantings at Rosemoor are particularly imaginative. To the north and east of this attractive house are slopes covered with rhododendrons and azaleas providing vivid colour in spring. The old tennis court now houses a fascinating collection of dwarf conifers, the stable yard tender plants: *Pittosporum tenuifolium*, the yellow climbing daisy (*Senecio scandens*), *Cleyera fortunei* 'Variegata' from Japan, and *Illicium floridanum* from America's deep south. Also close to the house are some interesting scree-covered beds accommodating plants from New Zealand, including the spiny *Aciphylla subflabellata* and the world's smallest conifer, *Dacrydium laxifolium*, which has bronze-grey foliage. There is a heather garden, too, and in the stone garden you will find some rare forms of camellia, including *C.* × *williamsii* 'St Ewe' which bears single pink flowers over a long season, and a rare mountain peony, *Paeonia suffruticosa* 'Rock's Variety'.

1 mile (1.5 km) south-east of Great Torrington,
on the B3220 (map page 58)

◆

ROUSHAM PARK OXFORDSHIRE

Rousham's garden is a perfect place of pilgrimage for students of the work of William Kent, for its landscape has remained virtually untouched since he created it in the early 18th century. Curving round the River Cherwell, which forms one of its boundaries, it has all the ingredients of the landscape style, with a splendid display of garden ornament and architecture. There are classical statues (ranging from a dying gladiator to Bacchus), ponds, *trompe-l'oeil* cascades, 'rustic' stonework, and lead swans in Venus' Vale. More waterworks can be seen at the Cold Bath, linked by a tiny stream to an octagonal pond. But the most impressive feature of all is an arcaded portico, the Praeneste, overlooking the river and the countryside beyond. There is a 'rustic' Doric temple, too, and on the skyline an eyecatcher, a sham ruin consisting of a flat wall pierced by three arches.

William Kent created the garden at Rousham Park

It is important to view the garden the way Kent intended you to, starting at the terrace, descending into Venus' Vale with its two pools linked by cascades, then taking the woodland path, with a serpentine rill to the Cold Bath and Townsend's Building with a vast cedar of Lebanon behind it. From here turn down the path to the statue of Apollo, then follow the lime walk, at the end of which the Praeneste comes into view. This brings you up towards the house and, eventually, to the pyramid building and the walled garden, which, amidst all this splendour, should not be missed. The scale is more domestic here, with herbaceous borders, a small parterre and espalier apple trees.

12 miles (19 km) north of Oxford, off
the A423 (map page 59)

◆

Topiary and statuary at Saling Hall

SALING HALL ESSEX

This is the place to see trees, not surprisingly, since it is the home of Hugh Johnson, author of *The International Book of Trees*. He has done some extensive work since taking over this 17th-century house and 12 acres (5 ha), clearing land and planting an arboretum of rare ornamental trees. The saplings here include cherries, willows, sorbus and some unusual birches.

In contrast to all this is the more domestic scale of the walled garden with its box edging enclosing an eclectic mixture of plants, sprawling roses and umbrella-shaped apple trees. Here Mediterranean plants thrive in the shelter of the walls; there are bulbs in spring and herbs in keeping with the garden's age (it dates from the late 1600s). The kitchen garden is worth a visit, too, for there are unusual vegetables growing there, notably Japanese salad ones. A large amelanchier, whose leaves turn ruby in the autumn, shades a bark garden where there are other unusual plants – *Paeonia delavayi*, for example, and *Hydrangea quercifolia* with its oak-leaf shaped leaves.

The Johnsons also plan a 'tea garden' featuring *Camellia sinensis*, the tea plant which they brought back from Georgia in the USSR. Continuing the oriental theme, they already have a waterfall in the style of a garden in Kyoto, Japan, and a dark-grey bronze Shinto arch and some stone snow lanterns. In addition, there is a splendid rose glade filled with pink shrub roses, including fine specimens of *Rosa gallica* 'Complicata' and *R.* 'Glauca', and through a grove of Norway maples is the water garden with moisture-loving plants like the giant huge-leaved *Gunnera manicata* dominating the scene; there is also a willow-fringed duck pond.

Notice, too, the five different vines that cover the front of Saling Hall, and the impressive avenue of Lombardy poplars, in the French style, leading up to the house.

In the village of Great Saling, 3 miles (5 km) west of Braintree, on the A120 (map page 59)

SAVILL GARDEN SURREY

Begun in 1932, this fine woodland garden set in 35 acres (14 ha) of Windsor Great Park is crammed with rhododendrons, camellias, magnolias and hydrangeas, backed by a host of other trees and shrubs. But it is the rhododendrons which form the backbone of the garden. The collection includes not only hardy but tender versions too, which can be seen in the Temperate House. The garden provides plenty of ideas on plantings for most woodland conditions: there is an extensive display of ferns, hostas, the beautiful blue poppy-like *Meconopsis grandis*, and primulas in plenty. There is something of colour and interest throughout the whole season. Go in spring for the daffodils and, of course, the rhododendrons, and in summer for the magnificent lilies. In September look out for the sudden dramatic appearance of autumn crocuses (colchicums), their heavy heads nodding on bare stems; they are followed later in the autumn by a firework display of golds, flames and crimsons from liquidambar trees, Japanese maples, sorbus, fothergillas and others.

There is also an impressive display of modern roses, some extensive herbaceous borders and, in contrast to the damp woodland, a very attractive dry garden – a recent addition, featuring plants from the Mediterranean and further afield. The lakes which lace the gardens are not natural but were created artificially as part of an elaborate drainage scheme by the Dukes of Cumberland in the late 1700s, when Windsor Park was nothing more than a wasteland of bog and heath. This work was continued by Eric Savill, a Deputy Park Ranger after whom the garden is named. Around the lakes you will find waterside plantings of *Iris laevigata* and the golden-leaved *Iris pseudacorus*, together with the more homely marsh marigold (*Caltha palustris*) and, on the foliage front, the water-loving royal fern and the magnificent *Gunnera manicata*.

On the eastern edge of Windsor Great Park, 5 miles (8 km) from Windsor, off the A30 (map page 59)

Scotney Castle   Kent

The owners of Scotney Castle, the Hussey family, decided in 1835 that they would rather look at the building than live in it, and promptly built themselves a new mansion up on the hill. The gardens were laid out around that time by William Sawrey Gilpin, borrowing heavily from the ideas of William Kent in reaction to 'Capability' Brown's spartan vistas, and the result is one of the most romantic gardens in this country.

A huge hole was blasted into the hillside for the new neo-Gothic villa, and the ever-practical Gilpin turned the debris into a vast quarry garden. Here he planted magnolias, rhododendrons and azaleas. He also persuaded the Hussey family to demolish part of the Elizabethan manor house which was attached to the castle, turning it into a ruined backdrop for his plantings, particularly climbers, roses and a white form of wisteria. The gardens at Scotney are a delight to visit at any time of year. There is a rose garden in the grounds of the castle, a small garden of herbs and old cottage plants in the courtyard, and little paths down the hill among trees and shrubs, from which you will see splendid views of the countryside beyond. A good place to visit, incidentally, if you have to garden on a slope.

$1\frac{1}{2}$ miles (2.5 km) south of
Lamberhurst, on the A21
(map page 59)

Shakespearian Gardens   Warwickshire

This is not one, but a series of gardens in and around Stratford-upon-Avon, linked with the life of William Shakespeare. The first, at his birthplace in Henley Street, is laid out as an association garden in memory of the poet: a lawn broken up by trees here and there, and borders planted with herbs and flowers mentioned in his works. Here you will find camomile, thyme, fennel and saffron – 'hot lavender, mints, savory, marjoram', too.

Left Azaleas and rhododendrons at Scotney Castle

Hall's Croft – one of the Shakespearian properties

Anne Hathaway's cottage garden at Shottery, $1\frac{1}{2}$ miles (2.5 km) away, is a typical cottage garden fringed by clipped box hedges and shrubs, and including 'bold oxlips and the crown imperial' and rosemary 'for remembrance', as well as daisies, violets and primroses – country flowers.

When Shakespeare retired from London and the theatre, he settled at New Place, a spacious property at that time. Only its foundations are left now, preserved in a setting of the Great Garden, as it is called – an expanse of perfect lawn with its splendid beech, and a very old mulberry tree said to have been grown from a cutting of a tree planted by the bard himself. There is a yew hedge here, set into compartments in which are old-fashioned flowers such as thistles, canterbury bells, hollyhocks and larkspur. The Knott Garden, which takes up part of the

site of the garden Shakespeare himself tended, is a relatively recent replica of an enclosed Elizabethan garden, modelled on designs and views shown in contemporary gardening books. It consists of four 'Knotts', or beds, each with an intricate pattern of clipped box interlaced with savory, hyssop, santolina and thyme. The spaces between are filled with bright bedding flowers.

Other gardens are to be found at Mary Arden's House, where Shakespeare's mother lived, and Hall's Croft, the home of Shakespeare's daughter and her husband. Taken together, they make a pleasant day out.

Situated in and around Stratford-
upon-Avon (map page 59)

◆

SHEFFIELD PARK   EAST SUSSEX

This is the definitive tree and shrub garden, not far from London in the East Sussex countryside. And autumn is the time to see it at its best, when the swamp cypresses have turned bronze, the birches yellow and the maples a blazing crimson. Then there is more colour from the amelanchiers, the parrotias, fothergillas and colour-barked cornus. But what most people come to see at this time of year are probably the tupelo trees (*Nyssa sylvatica*) at the edge of the lake with their beautiful golden leaves, and at their feet the blue of gentians and autumn crocuses.

'Capability' Brown and later Humphry Repton were responsible for the original design, creating more lakes (there are five in all) and planting clumps of trees here and there. But neither of them can take credit for the magnificent display we see today – that goes to Arthur G. Soames who bought Sheffield Park in 1909, and set to work planting the 140 acres (56 ha) with an imaginative mixture of trees.

Autumn is not the only time to visit this place. Go in spring for the sea of bluebells and wild flowers under the silver birches, and in May and June for bold splashes of colour from the rhododendrons and azaleas, the kalmias and

Left Vivid azaleas decorate the grounds at Sheffield Park

the cherries. In summer there are more flowering shrubs, water-lilies on the lakes, and lush waterside plants such as the gigantic gunnera.

5 miles (8 km) north-west of Uckfield,
on the A275 (map page 59)

◆

SHUGBOROUGH   STAFFORDSHIRE

Set on the edge of Cannock Chase, Shugborough, home of the Earl of Lichfield, boasts 900 acres (360 ha) of land in all, including an impressive landscaped park. Of special interest, however, is the series of eight monuments created in neo-classical style by Thomas Wright of Durham and James 'Athenian' Stewart, built in the mid 18th century. The historic ornamental garden covers some 22 acres (9 ha), and contains such neo-classical follies as the Ruin, built in 1750 beside the River Sow, and the Chinese House, with its curved roof. This is surrounded, appropriately, by Chinese trees and shrubs such as the Chinese necklace poplar (*Populus lasiocarpa*), peonies and bamboo. Standing nearby is what is claimed to be the largest yew tree in the country. The Shepherd's Monument, not far away, is skirted by shrub beds containing mahonia, cotoneaster, hosta and philadelphus. Follow the serpentine paths through the classical and Victorian gardens and you will come to a very pretty rose garden, designed in the 1960s by Graham Stuart Thomas.

In 1975, the present Lord Lichfield started a collection of unusual species of oaks in the arboretum on an island on a bend of the River Sow. There are now over 50 species, among them the red oak from North America, the European weeping oak, the Caucasian oak from the USSR and the Daimio oak, with its spectacular 1 ft (30 cm) long leaves, from north-east Asia and Japan.

6 miles (9.5 km) east of Stafford, off the
A513 (map pages 58–9)

◆

Guided Tour

SISSINGHURST CASTLE   KENT
Despite the death of its famous owner, gardening writer Vita Sackville-West, in 1962, Sissinghurst remains one of the most intensely personal gardens in this country. Opened to the public for the first time under the National Gardens Scheme on 1 May 1938, it is now hideously overcrowded at popular times of the year, when hordes tramp through the grounds. Despite that, it remains a place that every passionate gardener should visit at least once in a lifetime.

Its history is well documented. Most people know by now how Vita and Harold Nicolson found the castle (which dates from the reign of Henry VIII) and its neglected grounds and turned it into the most romantic garden of the century. Vita always denied that she was influenced by HIDCOTE MANOR (Gloucestershire) when she designed Sissinghurst (indeed, it was Harold Nicolson who drew up the ground plan). But the two gardens do have a similar theme of outdoor 'rooms', and it is the way in which it is divided into enclosures that gives Sissinghurst such a domestic scale. Any visitor goes away full of ideas for his own garden, however small.

You enter Sissinghurst through an archway leading into the courtyard with its tall yews standing sentinel, the long-flowering 'Allen Chandler' rose around the entrance arch and a purple border along the north wall. In front of you is Vita's famous tower and the room where she wrote. Climb this for a panoramic view of the garden as a whole and to get your bearings.

Cross the lawn of the tower garden behind it, and on your right is the rondel, planted in the 1930s. Here immaculate hedges surround rose beds which contain Vita's huge collection of old-fashioned climbing and shrub roses, with under-plantings of alliums and, in spring, irises. Many of the roses have heavy, almost brooding colours, ranging from the crimson velvety *Rosa gallica* 'Tuscany' and almost purple 'Cardinal de Richelieu' and 'William Lobb' to the near black 'Souvenir du Docteur Jamain'. Vita said that they should 'be allowed to ramp away into big bushes' and that is what they have done.

Beyond it is the lime walk with its pleached trees edged in spring with fritillaries, anemones, grape hyacinths, tulips, and bulbs of all kinds. On the left is Delos, described by Vita as 'an unconventional sort of rock garden, inspired by the Island

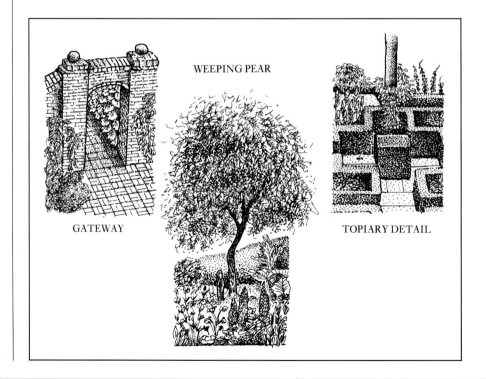

GATEWAY

WEEPING PEAR

TOPIARY DETAIL

Looking down from the tower at Sissinghurst to the yew walk and the cottage garden

of Delos', next to the Priest's House. In front lies the famous, much copied white garden with its box-edged beds full of white, grey and silver plants, and its metal frame designed by Harold Nicolson, and covered in *Rosa longicuspis*, in the centre. In spring 'White Triumphator' tulips emerge through the silvery *Lamium maculatum album*, to be followed by lilies and roses in profusion – 'Iceberg', for example – and on one side stands a weeping pear with a statue beneath it.

The yew walk runs from north to south across these gardens with the orchard beyond. Here is one of the earliest wild-flower gardens, with spring bulbs naturalized in the grass. The moat walk, to the right of the orchard, is fringed by the nuttery which in Vita's day was carpeted with rainbow-coloured polyanthus and now has euphorbias, hardy geraniums and sweet woodruff around the bases of the trees, as the polyanthus had improverished the soil to the extent that it was time for a change. Tucked away in the top right-hand corner, reached via a thyme lawn, is the famous herb garden which Vita Sackville-West planted with over 60 different varieties, mainly for their foliage, as she was not a keen cook. Today it is one of the most visited areas at Sissinghurst.

1 mile (1.5 km) north-east of Sissinghurst, on the A262
(map page 59)

SIZERGH CASTLE   CUMBRIA

Sizergh has a rock garden in the grand tradition. It covers three-quarters of an acre (0.3 ha), and it is said that it took a team of horses and eight men to haul the huge pieces of local limestone into position. At the time when Lord Strickland ordered it from T.R. Hayes' nursery at nearby Ambleside, rock gardens were all the rage, but this one was built in a great hollow gouged out of the side of the hill and watched over by a 14th-century pele tower covered with Boston ivy. The years have mellowed it, and it is difficult to think of it as anything other than a natural phenomenon now. But the planting is spectacular. Apart from traditional alpine plants such as gentians and primulas, one of the National Collections of Hardy Ferns is kept here, making a splendid setting for the tiny flowers. Over the years what were originally dwarf conifers have grown surprisingly large and stand up like bizarre exclamation marks among the lower-growing shrubs.

Sizergh also has a wild-flower bank of great beauty – look for the spring bulbs, the ox-eye daisies and then the butterfly orchids in June. The cleverly planted herbaceous border is well worth a visit in summer, as is the rose garden where climbers intertwine with clematis and shrub roses are underplanted with hardy geraniums and *Lamium maculatum* 'Beacon Silver'. In autumn go for the red-gold tints, as the Japanese maples and some of the climbers turn crimson.

3½ miles (5.5 km) south of Kendal, on
the A591 (map page 60)

◆

STOURHEAD   WILTSHIRE

The house at Stourhead was designed in 1721 for the banker Henry Hoare, whose son Henry laid out the 'pleasure grounds' from 1741 onwards, damming several medieval fishponds to make a series of lakes – and pleasure grounds they remain, rather than gardens in a domestic sense. Henry Hoare also planted a belt of forest trees along the combe top to protect the garden from the winter wind that blows from Salisbury Plain, creating a tree-lined ride

Stourhead's gardens, designed by the Hoare family

round the perimeter of the park with spectacular views of the valley. The gardens are adorned by wonderful buildings: temples, obelisks and a grotto. In 1744 Hoare built the Temple of Flora above a spring, and the elegant Pantheon dominates the estate, commanding attention from every point in the garden. Today the garden is generally agreed to be among the finest examples of an 18th-century landscape, though no famous name is attached to its design.

Henry Hoare used a broad canvas and the most interesting plantings are of trees and shrubs rather than flowers. There was much further planting in the 19th and 20th centuries, and today the shores and lower woodlands contain magnificent specimens of conifers, tulip trees, beeches, plane trees, swamp cypresses, dawn redwoods, Indian bean trees, and rhododendrons, including many rarities. Stourhead is beautiful throughout the year but probably at its best in May when the chestnut trees and the rhododendrons show their colour. Or again in the autumn, lit by the golden leaves of lime trees and the flame-red of the maples. It is laid out on a grand scale, but despite the huge variety of fine trees, it is the man-made things – the temples, obelisks and statuary – which ultimately dominate the scene.

3 miles (5 km) north-west of Mere, off
the B3092 (map pages 58–9)

◆

Looking across water to the Temple of Ancient Virtue at Stowe

STOWE LANDSCAPE GARDENS
BUCKINGHAMSHIRE

All of the leading landscape designers of their day – Bridgeman, Vanbrugh, Kent, Gibbs and Brown – had a hand in this garden which was started by Viscount Cobham in the 1700s. Cobham wanted an idyllic retreat for his family and political friends, and he attacked the project with great passion, spending 40 years and a great deal of his wealth to achieve his aims. Later additions to the house and garden were made by other members of the family, the Dukes of Buckingham and Chandos. But disaster struck: in 1848 bankruptcy led to the sale of the contents of the house, and despite efforts to save it, the estate was sold in 1921 and the house turned into a school. However, in 1989 the National Trust acquired the gardens.

Stowe is an 18th-century paradise and the gardens retain much of their original grandeur. In addition to 'Capability' Brown's Arcadian rolling lawns, woods and placid lakes in the new naturalistic style of the period, there are an enormous number of garden buildings to see – more than 30 in all: temples, obelisks, pillars, a grotto, and the imposing shell bridge, designed by William Kent, which is not a bridge at all, but an ornate pedimented arcade with a cascade in the centre. There are some fine trees, but the landscape is on too grand a scale for small shrubs or flowers. To walk through Kent's exquisite, carefully planted valley, dubbed the Elysian Fields, is an experience in itself.

2 miles (3 km) north-west of
Buckingham, off the A422
(map page 59)

◆

STUDLEY ROYAL PARK   NORTH YORKSHIRE

In 1722 John Aislabie, once Chancellor of the Exchequer, retreated to his estate at Studley when he was bankrupted and disgraced in the South Sea Bubble affair, the great financial scandal of the day. Forced into early retirement, he put his talents to work to create a water garden which is now one of the most picturesque landscapes in the country. Aislabie set his garden out of sight of the house, so that when he walked around it no building intruded on the pastoral scene. He tackled a steep-sided valley, straightened the River Skell, turning the curves of the river into moon and crescent ponds and making part of it into a canal leading to a lake, then added fishing lodges at one end and temples dotted on the hillside.

When Aislabie died, his son took over the task of finishing the gardens, incorporating the idea, perfected by the Chinese, of using 'borrowed' scenery. He aligned the principal avenue on Ripon Minster, so that its towers could be seen in the distance, and bought Fountains Abbey, further down the valley, in order to incorporate its ruins in the garden. If you can, take the marvellous walk right round the valley, see the splendidly overgrown grotto with water coursing from it, the moon and crescent ponds (which look their best seen from the thickly wooded hills above), and explore the ruins of the abbey on the way.

2 miles (3 km) west of Ripon, off the
B6265 (map page 60)

◆

SYON PARK   LONDON

This is a 'Capability' Brown garden, designed to match the splendour of Robert Adam's Syon House. Like all his gardens it is planned on a grandiose scale with woodlands which still contain some of the original trees, and two lakes now decorated with great clumps of Chilean rhubarb.

There are two main reasons for visiting Syon. The first is the magnificent domed conservatory which was built in 1827 for the Duke of Northumberland by Charles Fowler, architect of the covered market at old Covent Garden. It was designed at the time to be able to contain full-sized forest trees, and inspired Joseph Paxton to copy the idea at CHATSWORTH (Derbyshire). Today it has a collection of cacti in it, and some other unusual plants. Nearby is a formal garden with a pool and topiary. The second attraction at Syon is its rose garden, built on a 16th-century terrace, and covering 6 acres (2.4 ha). It contains roses of all kinds, more than 200 varieties, from standards and climbers to shrub roses. See them when they are at their best, in early summer. Syon's third attraction is a special plot for the disabled, showing what can be done, gardening from a wheelchair.

**2 miles (3 km) west of Kew Bridge, off
the A315 (map page 59)**

TINTINHULL HOUSE SOMERSET

This garden, which was designed in the 1930s and 1940s by Phyllis Reiss, an inspired plantswoman, is similar to SISSINGHURST CASTLE (Kent) and HIDCOTE MANOR (Gloucestershire) – HIDCOTE was Mrs Reiss's inspiration. Now tended by Penelope Hobhouse, the well-known gardening writer, it has a series of garden rooms, hedged or walled, each with a different theme and colour scheme. The result is some inspired planting aimed to give something of interest all year round. As the colour in one border fades, another takes over. It also shows how to tackle what is essentially a long narrow plot. The grounds cover 1 acre

Tintinhull House garden, designed in the 1930s and 1940s

(0.4 ha) in all, and the main feature is three garden rooms: Eagle Court, Middle Garden and Fountain Garden which run directly behind the house. Ranged down one side is a lawned area, Cedar Court, a long rectangular pool and loggia, and the kitchen garden.

It is the borders that you go to see at Tintinhull. Most of them are mixed, composed of shrubs, flowering and foliage plants, grasses and bulbs. And it is the mixture that makes them so interesting and so visually appealing. One area is filled with purple-leaved prunus and other coppery shrubs and plants, together with roses, phloxes and asters, all contributing crimson, purple and pink colourings. Another area, round the small fountain pool, is devoted to cool white flowers and grey-leaved plants.

This is a formal garden with freestyle planting, and a useful plant list tells you exactly what is growing where.

**5 miles (8 km) north-west of Yeovil,
south of the A303 (map pages 58–9)**

TRADESCANT GARDEN LONDON

Here is an inner city garden, a quiet oasis near a roundabout of swirling traffic on the south bank of the River Thames. The Tradescants, father and son, 17th-century gardeners successively to Lord Salisbury, the Duke of Buckingham and Charles I, brought back from their travels abroad many of the plants we take for granted today. These were propagated in their famous garden in Lambeth, and both Tradescants are buried in a tomb (alongside that of Captain Bligh of the *Bounty*) in the churchyard of St Mary-at-Lambeth, next to Lambeth Palace. Part of the churchyard has now been designed as an enchanting replica of a 17th-century garden, containing plants known to have been grown by the Tradescants together with other plants of the period. The church itself, meanwhile, has become a museum of garden history.

The main feature is a pretty knot garden, completed in 1983, which is relatively small in scale and could easily be copied to fit an average back garden. The knot itself is made with a mixture of box and santolina, while the centre-piece is the holly *Ilex aquifolium* 'Silver King'. All the main herbs are used, but many are in unusual forms – a furry-leaved lavender, a golden-leaved oregano, a three-coloured sage (*Salvia officinalis* 'Tricolor') and a white variety of hyssop. A number of little species bulbs are there, such as *Narcissus triandrus albus*, and even the humble daisy has its place. The Tradescants were closely involved with the gardens at HATFIELD HOUSE (Hertfordshire), so it was fitting that this knot garden was planned by Lady Salisbury who has also planted a memorial garden at HATFIELD HOUSE itself, in their memory.

**The Museum of Garden History at St
Mary-at-Lambeth, on Lambeth Palace
Road, SE1 (map page 59)**

◆

TRESCO ABBEY GARDEN   ISLES OF SCILLY

This amazing, lush garden has been formed on a small island out in the Atlantic, in a climate that is exceptionally windy as well as being exceptionally mild. It was developed back in 1834 by Augustus Smith who settled on Tresco from Hertfordshire, moving into a disused priory there. He began by constructing a series of walled enclosures around the ruins, then windbreaks to protect his first plantings from the severe salt-bearing gales. The result was startling – he had managed to create a microclimate that resulted in a remarkable garden full of exotic plants, many of Mediterranean origin, and even succulents which grew and flowered outdoors for the first time in the British Isles.

By 1850, news of the garden had spread, and intrepid travellers arrived to see it, ringing the bell on the gate at Valhalla, the rugged stone house that Smith had built. He was succeeded by generations of the Dorrien-Smith family, who have developed the gardens to their present state of perfection, complete with the only garden heliport in the world, allowing mainland visitors to be delivered almost to the garden gate. You would be forgiven for thinking that you had arrived on an island in the South, rather than the North Atlantic. There is a great deal to see here – some notable palms, for instance, such as the cabbage tree palm (*Cordyline australis* 'Lentiginosa') from New Zealand, which grows to a great height, and huge tree ferns from the same country. The protea from South Africa, much loved by flower arrangers, grows here too, out of doors. Each member of the Dorrien-Smith family has in turn contributed plants from different parts of the world, and this exciting collection is the result of their labours.

**On the island of Tresco, by car ferry or
the passenger-only helicopter service
from Penzance (map page 58)**

◆

TREWITHEN HOUSE   CORNWALL

Spring is the time to visit Trewithen, when the marvellous magnolias are in flower. Their spectacular size, and the colours – pinks and purples offset by white – make them an unforgettable sight. Presiding over the whole display is the most impressive of them all, a huge *Magnolia cambellii mollicomata* on the right-hand side of the lawn.

The garden was made by George Johnstone, who inherited it in 1904 and found that the house was almost entirely surrounded by trees. During World War I, however, a large number of these were felled for vitally needed timber, and this gave Johnstone the chance to design a new garden for himself, stretching away from the south front of the house. Here he made a lawn and a woodland which he filled with magnolias, camellias and rhododendrons.

Despite being crippled in a hunting accident in the 1930s, Johnstone not only sought after but also bred some remarkable plants. Look for *Rhododendron hunnewellianum* 'Alison Johnstone' and *Camellia* 'Alison Johnstone', named after his wife. There are many others, notably *Camellia saluenensis* 'Trewithen Red', *C. japonica* 'Trewithen White', and *Ceanothus arboreus* 'Trewithen Blue'. Apart from the obvious delights, there are many fascinating trees and shrubs from South America, New Zealand, China and all over the world. There is a water garden, and the old walled garden where Johnstone once complained that the colours depended on 'the shades of washing hung out by the maids' is now planted with roses, and has a bright border.

**Between Truro and St Austell, on the
A390 (map page 58)**

◆

WATERPERRY GARDENS OXFORDSHIRE

These gardens grew out of a training college and now house a thriving garden centre and shop. Waterperry was founded in the 1930s by a Miss Havergal as a horticultural training college for young ladies. The college is no more but the buildings are still used for day release and amateur courses in gardening, and the ornamental gardens are still worth a visit.

The pride of Waterperry is its magnificent herbaceous border backed by a red-brick wall which leads down through a rock garden and lawns shaded by majestic trees to a tributary of the Thames, the River Thame. The border is at its most colourful in June and July, with a second burst when the asters come out in autumn. The rock garden has interesting dwarf conifers, – a *Picea albertiana* 'Conica', for instance, and the cigar-shaped *Juniperus communis* 'Compressa'. Two other interesting conifers are the well-established *Chamaecyparis tamariskifolia* and the *Thuya occidentalis* 'Rheingold'. The upper path of the rock garden leads to a small woodland area, Sebb's Corner, where Christmas roses and snowdrops can be found in winter, together with the strange yellow-green flowerheads of *Petasites japonicus*. In the corner is a *Metasequoia glyptostroboides*, once thought to be extinct but rediscovered in 1947. A great deal of soft fruit is grown at Waterperry, and it is a delight to walk through the disciplined ranks of loganberries, blackberries and raspberries.

**8 miles (13 km) east of Oxford, off the
M40/A40 (map page 59)**

◆

The landscaped grounds of West Wycombe Park

WEST WYCOMBE PARK BUCKINGHAMSHIRE

Essentially 4000 acres (1600 ha) of parkland, rather than a garden, West Wycombe surrounds a fine Palladian mansion built in the mid 18th century. The landscaped grounds were the creation of Sir Francis Dashwood, the 2nd Baronet, who, in common with most aristocrats of that time, went on a series of Grand Tours in the early 1700s. Impressed by what he saw, he decided to create what has been described as one of the most perfect expressions in this country of the 'natural landscape' school of gardening. A stream was dammed to make the great lake, and a Broad Walk was laid out to the west of it, with serpentine streams and paths in the woods on either side. The Cascade which has been restored in recent years has two splendid reclining figures on flint plinths on either side – in fact, these are fibreglass copies of the original lead statues, though they look absolutely authentic. In common with other gardens of the period, there are a number of set pieces: the Temple of the Winds, for instance, and the Music Temple on the island, with its elegant Doric colonnade, designed as a place for masques and *fêtes-champêtres*. A fleet of four vessels was kept on the lake, to engage in mock naval battles and amuse Sir Francis's guests. Kitty's Lodge and Daphne's Temple flank the entrance to the main drive. The Temple of Apollo, next to the south front, has a room above it that once held a sandpit and cages for cock fighting. At one time Thomas Cook, a pupil of 'Capability' Brown, was involved in work at West Wycombe, and Humphry Repton also lent a hand at one time, thinning out some of the overgrown clumps of trees. Now new planting and restoration has been undertaken by the National Trust.

To the south of West Wycombe, off the
A40 (map page 59)

◆

WILTON HOUSE   WILTSHIRE

The impressive triumphal arch erected by Sir William Chambers at Wilton in 1755 hints at some of the splendours that used to be seen beyond. It has, on the top, a copy of the bronze statue of Marcus Aurelius on horseback outside the Capitol in Rome. But alas, most of the gardens that went with it have now all but disappeared, leaving only some statuary behind.

In the 1600s the Palladian architecture of the south front had a classical garden to go with it, stretching across the whole width of the house. It was designed by the then-fashionable landscape artist Isaac de Caus. De Caus also dammed the little River Wylye to make one of the first ornamental cascades in England, with lipped ledges to catch the light in the water and make rainbows. Today, however, Wilton offers nothing much more than a park to walk in. There is a very elegant Palladian bridge based, like that at STOWE (Buckinghamshire), on a plan for the Rialto in Venice which was never executed. Lead putti alternate with urns on the terrace on the west side, but this is not open to the public. However, new things are happening at Wilton. A large rose garden has been made with a good collection of old-fashioned roses, and a new water garden is planned. Meanwhile, you can see some of the original statues in the front courtyard of the house, which is decorated with lavender and lime trees and has a fountain as a centrepiece.

2½ miles (4 km) west of Salisbury, on
the A30 (map page 59)

◆

WISLEY GARDEN   SURREY

Here is the garden for gardeners, *par excellence*: you come to admire but also to learn. The 250 acres (100 ha) reflect the highest possible standards of all types of gardening. They are immaculately kept, wide-ranging in content, and a constant source of inspiration. Famous for its hardy shrubs and demonstration gardens, Wisley can be depended on to have something worth seeing every month of the year, from a display of shrubs for winter effect in January to herbaceous borders, lilies and summer bedding plants in the walled garden in August.

The garden was begun by G.F. Wilson in the 1870s and given to the Royal Horticultural Society by Sir Thomas Hanbury (creator of the famous Italian garden La Mortola) in 1903. The house is now used for offices and laboratories, and the gardens immediately around it are predominantly formal, though the planting is relaxed. Terraced lawns are softened by tender wall shrubs and climbers – you will see the pink-and-cream-splashed foliage of an *Actinidia kolomikta*, for instance, and more than one kind of ceanothus. Two walled gardens nearby were designed by Geoffrey Jellicoe and Lanning Roper: one contains a parterre, the other a fountain surrounded by old-fashioned roses and silver-leaved plants.

There is an alpine meadow full of wild flowers and bulbs in spring, and a colourful display of moisture-loving plants by the banks of the stream which separates the woodland and the rock garden. The rock garden is one of the most impressive in England, and in the alpine house above it you

Wisley – home to the Royal Horticultural Society

can admire specimens at close quarters. Hidden behind high hedges are the model vegetable gardens familiar to anyone who watched the television programmes filmed here. You will also find an ornamental herb garden, displays of annuals in island beds and a pool with aquatic plants.

4 miles (6.5 km) south-west of Cobham, on the A3 (map page 59)

WOLSELEY GARDEN PARK STAFFORDSHIRE

This is a brand-new garden park created by Sir Charles and Lady Wolseley on grounds bordering the River Trent. Wolseley Hall itself was demolished in 1967, but Sir Charles, who at one time managed the Rothschild family's gardens at EXBURY (Hampshire), is now developing the estate as a tourist attraction: some 1300 acres (520 ha) have been transformed into a series of 15 or more theme gardens. The existing grounds included mature trees and shrubs, a lake, a stream and two ponds. Within this framework Sir Charles has already planted a 2-acre (0.8 ha) walled rose garden with a strong historic theme; it contains more than 4000 roses ranging from those known in medieval times to the introductions of the present day. There is also a water and bog garden, a woodland spring garden, and a rockery with a scree bed. A scented garden designed especially for blind or partially-sighted visitors is already in place, while Irish yews and western red cedars enclose a cathedral garden.

A pretty bridal walk of white-flowering trees and shrubs and a weeping garden, featuring trees and shrubs of a pendulous habit mirrored in a pond, were planted in 1990, and there is a new American garden modelled on those planted by the first settlers in Virginia. There are silver and gold gardens, a large maze in the shape of mainland Britain, and the figures in the children's topiary garden are modelled on characters from A.A. Milne.

2 miles (3 km) north of Rugeley, on the A51 (map pages 58–9)

WREST PARK BEDFORDSHIRE

The gardens at Wrest Park provide a fascinating example of the changing styles of gardening fashionable in England between 1700 and 1850. The impressive Great Garden was laid out in semi-formal manner early in the 18th century, and is dominated by the Long Water, a magnificent canal with a fine pavilion at its south end. On either side are hedge-lined alleys and walks giving on to enclosures containing monuments and ornaments from the period. Although 'Capability' Brown was called in to 'improve' and naturalize the landscape, much of the early 18th-century garden remains untouched. He did turn some of the original canals into a river which snakes round the property, but the 18th-century bowling-green house, the rustic bath house, a Chinese bridge and a pagan altar are all still there.

When the old house was pulled down in the early 1830s and a new one built on fashionable French château lines, Earl de Grey left the original gardens virtually intact but added the French garden with its statues and fountain in front of the new house. He also built the orangery.

East of Silsoe, off the A6 (map page 59)

Opening Times

—◆—

Note Current opening times are given for the gardens listed in the gazetteer, but these may be subject to change. Before making a special journey to visit a particular garden, it may be best to check that it will be open. Where there is also a house open to the public, please note that its opening times are likely to vary from those of the garden.

ACORN BANK GARDEN
Easter to early November: daily 10–6
ALTON TOWERS
All year: daily 9–6/7/8 (depending on the time of year)
BARNSLEY HOUSE GARDEN
All year: Monday, Wednesday, Thursday and Saturday 10–6
BATEMAN'S
Easter to end October: daily (except Thursday and Friday) 11–5.30. Last admission 4.30 pm. Open bank holiday Monday and Good Friday
BENTHALL HALL
End March to end September: Wednesday, Sunday and bank holiday Monday 1.30–5.30
BETH CHATTO GARDENS
March to end October: Monday to Saturday 9–5. November to end February: Monday to Friday 9–4. Gardens and nursery closed every Sunday and bank holiday, and for two weeks over Christmas and the New Year

BICTON PARK
March and October: daily 10–4. Rest of year: daily 10–6
BIDDULPH GRANGE
May to early November: Wednesday to Friday 12–6; Saturday, Sunday and bank holiday Monday 11–6. Mid November to mid December: Saturday and Sunday only 12–4
BLENHEIM PALACE
Mid March to end October: daily 10.30–5.30. Last admission 4.45 pm
BODNANT GARDEN
Mid March to end October: daily 10–5
BOWOOD HOUSE
Mid March to early November: daily 11–6. Garden centre open daily 9–6 all year
BRANKLYN GARDEN
March to end October: daily 9.30–sunset
BRODICK CASTLE
All year: daily 9.30–sunset
BURFORD HOUSE GARDEN
Mid March to mid October: Monday

to Saturday 10–5; Sunday 1–5. From mid October to mid March the gardens are open Monday to Friday by appointment only
CAPEL MANOR
Easter to end October: daily 10–5.30. November to Easter: Monday to Friday only 10–4.30. Check opening times for public holidays
CASTLE DROGO
Easter to end September: daily 11–6. October: daily 11–5. Last admission half an hour before closing
CASTLE HOWARD
Mid March to early November: daily 10–4.30
CHATSWORTH
End March to early November: daily 11–5
CHELSEA PHYSIC GARDEN
Mid March to mid October: Wednesday and Sunday 2–5. In Chelsea Flower Show week, open Tuesday to Friday 12–5
CHENIES MANOR HOUSE
April to end October: Wednesday and Thursday 2–5. Also open May Day and summer bank holiday 2–6
CHIRK CASTLE
Easter to end September: daily (except Monday and Saturday) 12–6. Early October to early November: Saturday and Sunday only 12–6. Open bank holiday Monday 12–5
CHISWICK HOUSE
Good Friday or 1 April (whichever is earlier) to end September: daily 10–6. 1 October to Maundy Thursday or 31 March (whichever is earlier): daily 10–4. Closed 24–5 December

CLAREMONT
April to end October: daily 9–7.
November to end March 9–5 (or
sunset if earlier). Last admission half
an hour before closing. Closed
Christmas Day and New Year's Day

CLAVERTON MANOR
End March to early November: daily
(except Monday) 1–6

CLIVEDEN
March to end October: daily 11–6.
November and December:
daily 11–4

COMPTON ACRES
March to end October: daily
10.30–6.30

CORNWELL MANOR
Contact direct for details

CRATHES CASTLE
All year: daily 9.30–sunset

CULZEAN CASTLE
All year: daily 9–sunset

DENMANS
All year: daily 9–5. Closed 25–6
December

DYFFRYN BOTANIC GARDEN
Easter to October: daily 10.30–5.30

EASTGROVE COTTAGE GARDEN
April to July, and September to end
October: daily (except Tuesday and
Wednesday) 2–5. Closed in August

EAST LAMBROOK MANOR
Mid January to end October:
Monday to Saturday, and bank
holiday weekends 10–5

ERDDIG
Good Friday to mid October: daily
(except Thursday and Friday) 12–6

EXBURY GARDENS
First week of March to first week of
July: daily 10–5.30 (late opening

until 7.30 pm, or sunset if earlier, on
Tuesday and Wednesday). Second
week of July to mid September (only
half the gardens open): daily 10–5.30.
Mid September to end October:
daily 10–5.30 (or sunset if earlier)

FALKLAND PALACE
Easter or 1 April (whichever is
earlier) to end October: Monday to
Saturday 10–6; Sunday 2–6. Last
admission 5 pm

FARNBOROUGH HALL
April to end September: Wednesday
and Saturday 2–6 (Terrace Walk
only: Thursday and Friday 2–6).
Last admission 5.30 pm

GARSINGTON MANOR
Contact direct for details

GRAYTHWAITE HALL GARDENS
1 April to mid July: daily 10–6

GREAT DIXTER
End March to mid October: Tuesday
to Sunday, and bank holiday Monday
2–5. July and August: garden open
11–5 on Sunday

HADDON HALL
Good Friday to end September:
Tuesday to Sunday 11–6. Closed
Monday except bank holiday
Monday; also closed Sunday in July
and August except bank holiday
weekends

HAMPTON COURT PALACE
All year: daily 9.30–sunset

HARDWICK HALL
End March to end October: daily
12–5.30. Closed Good Friday

HATFIELD HOUSE
End March to mid October: Park –
daily (except Good Friday) 10.30–8;
West Gardens – daily (except Good

Friday) 11–6; East Gardens –
Monday only (except bank holiday
Monday) 2–5

HEVER CASTLE
Mid March to mid November: daily
11–6. Last admission 5 pm

HIDCOTE MANOR GARDEN
End March to end October: daily
(except Tuesday and Friday) 11–7
(or an hour before dusk if earlier)

HILL TOP
Easter to early November: Monday
to Wednesday, Saturday and Sunday
(closed Thursday and Friday, except
Good Friday) 11–5

HOLKER HALL
April to end October: daily (except
Saturday) 10.30–6

HOLKHAM HALL
Mid May to end September: daily
(except Friday and Saturday) 1.30–5.
Open 11.30–5 on Easter, May, spring
and summer bank holiday Sundays
and Mondays

HOWICK HALL
April to October: daily 2–7

IFORD MANOR
May to end September: Tuesday,
Wednesday, Thursday, Saturday,
Sunday and summer bank holidays
2–5. Also open Sundays in April and
October, and Easter Monday

INVEREWE GARDEN
All year: daily 9.30–sunset

ISABELLA PLANTATION
All year: open daily – summer
months 7–sunset; winter months
8–sunset

JENKYN PLACE
April to mid September: Thursday
to Sunday 2–6

KENSINGTON ROOF GARDEN
All year: Sunday 12.30–3. Available for private hire at other times – contact direct for details

KEW: ROYAL BOTANIC GARDENS
All year: open daily from 9.30 am. Closing times vary from 4 pm to 6.30 pm on weekdays and from 4 pm to 8 pm on Sundays and bank holidays, depending on the time of sunset. Closed 25 December and 1 January. Closing time also vary for glasshouses and galleries

KIFTSGATE COURT GARDEN
April to end September: Sunday, Wednesday, Thursday and bank holiday Monday 2–6

KNIGHTSHAYES COURT
April to end October: daily 11–6

KNOLE
Garden open May to September: first Wednesday in each month 11–5. Park open daily to pedestrians

LEONARDSLEE
Mid April to mid June: daily 10–6. Mid June to September: weekends only 10–6. October: weekends only 10–5

LEVENS HALL
All year: Sunday to Thursday 11–5

LONGLEAT
Easter to end September 10–6; rest of year 10–4. Closed Christmas Day. Safari Park open daily from mid March to end October 10–6. Last admission 5.30 pm (or sunset if earlier)

LUTON HOO
End March to mid October: daily (except Monday) 12–6. Open bank holiday Monday 10.30–6

MELBOURNE HALL
April to September: Wednesday, Saturday, Sunday and bank holiday Monday 2–6

MYDDELTON HOUSE
Weekdays (except bank holidays) 10–3. In addition there are 12 open Sundays throughout the year, and guided tours can be arranged

NYMANS GARDEN
End March to end October: daily (except Monday and Friday) 11–7 (or sunset if earlier). Open bank holiday Monday and Good Friday

PACKWOOD HOUSE
Easter to end September: Wednesday to Sunday, and bank holiday Monday 2–6. Closed Good Friday. October: Wednesday to Sunday 12.30–4.30

PAINSHILL PARK
Mid April to mid October: Sunday only 2–6. Last admission 5 pm. Pre-booked group visits may be arranged in advance for any day except Sunday

PARNHAM HOUSE
Easter or 1 April (whichever is earlier) to end October: Wednesday, Sunday and bank holidays 10–5. Tuesday and Thursday also available for pre-booked group visits

PENRHYN CASTLE
End March to early November: daily (except Tuesday) 11–6

PENSHURST PLACE
End March to end September: daily (except Monday) 12.30–6. Open all bank holidays in season

PITMEDDEN GARDEN
May to end September: daily 10–6. Last admission 5.15 pm

PLAS NEWYDD
End March to June, and September: daily (except Saturday) 12–5. July and August: daily (except Saturday) 11–5. October to early November: Friday and Sunday only 12–5.

POLESDEN LACEY
All year: daily 11–sunset

POWIS CASTLE
End March to end June: daily (except Monday and Tuesday) 11–6. July to end August: daily (except Monday) 11–6. September to early November: daily (except Monday and Tuesday) 11–6. Open bank holiday Monday. Early November to end March: Sunday only 2–4.30

THE PRIORY
May to September: Thursday only 2–7. Also open on selected Sundays throughout summer months. Contact direct for details

ROSEMOOR GARDEN
Open all year – contact direct for details

ROUSHAM PARK
All year: daily 10–4.30

SALING HALL
Open for the National Gardens Scheme, and at other times during the summer. Contact direct for details

SAVILL GARDEN
All year: Monday to Friday 10–6 (or sunset if earlier); weekends 10–7 (or sunset if earlier). Closed at Christmas

SCOTNEY CASTLE
April to mid November: Wednesday to Friday 11–6 (or sunset if earlier); Saturday, Sunday and bank holiday

Monday 2–6 (or sunset if earlier).
Closed Good Friday. Last admission
half an hour before closing
SHAKESPEARIAN GARDENS
All the properties open daily all year,
except Good Friday morning, 24–6
December, and 1 January morning
SHEFFIELD PARK
End March to mid November:
Tuesday to Saturday (closed Good
Friday) 11–6 (or sunset if earlier);
Sunday and bank holiday Monday
2–6 (or sunset if earlier). Sundays in
October and November 1–sunset.
Closed Tuesday following bank
holiday
SHUGBOROUGH
Easter to end October: daily 11–5.
End October to Easter: booked
parties only
SISSINGHURST CASTLE
Easter to mid October: Tuesday to
Friday 1–6.30; Saturday, Sunday
and Good Friday 10–6.30. Last
admission 6 pm. Closed Monday,
including bank holidays
SIZERGH CASTLE
End March to end October:
Sunday to Thursday 12.30–5.30.
Last admission 5 pm. Closed
Good Friday
STOURHEAD
All year: daily 8–7 (or sunset if
earlier)

STOWE LANDSCAPE GARDENS
Open only during school holidays:
daily 10–6 (or sunset if earlier). Last
admission an hour before closing.
Closed Good Friday and 25–6
December
STUDLEY ROYAL PARK
April to June: daily 10–7. July and
August: daily 10–8. September: daily
10–7. October: daily 10–6 (or sunset
if earlier). November to March: 10–5
(or sunset if earlier). Closed 24–5
December
SYON PARK
All year: daily 10–6 (or sunset if
earlier). Last admission an hour
before closing. Closed 25–6
December
TINTINHULL HOUSE
April to end September: Wednesday,
Thursday and Saturday (also open
bank holiday Monday) 2–6
TRADESCANT GARDEN
First Sunday in March to second
Sunday in December: Monday to
Friday 11–3; Sunday 10.30–5
TRESCO ABBEY GARDEN
All year: daily 10–4
TREWITHEN HOUSE
March to end September: Monday to
Saturday (closed Sunday) 10–4.30
WATERPERRY GARDENS
April to September: Monday to
Friday 10–5.30; weekends 10–6.

October to March: daily 10–4.30.
Closed during Christmas and New
Year holidays
WEST WYCOMBE PARK
April and May: Sunday and
Wednesday 2–6, and Easter, May
Day and spring bank holidays 2–6.
Closed Good Friday. June, July and
August: Sunday to Thursday, and
summer bank holiday 2–6. Last
admission 5.15 pm
WILTON HOUSE
Easter to mid October: Tuesday to
Saturday and bank holiday Monday
11–6; Sunday 12.30–6
WISLEY GARDEN
February to October: Monday to
Saturday 10–7 (or sunset if earlier).
November to January: Monday to
Saturday 10–4.30 (or sunset if
earlier). All year: open Sunday to
members of RHS and their guests
only. Glasshouses close Monday to
Friday at 4.15 pm (or sunset if
earlier); close weekends and bank
holidays at 4.45 pm (or sunset if
earlier)
WOLSELEY GARDEN PARK
Times vary seasonally, but open 10–6
in summer
WREST PARK
Good Friday or 1 April (whichever is
earlier) to end September: weekends
and bank holidays only 10–6

Glossary of Terms

◆

allée a French word, introduced into England in the 17th century, meaning a walk or avenue, sometimes lined with tall trees or clipped hedges

alpine strictly speaking, a plant that in its natural habitat grows in alpine or mountain conditions. The term is now also used to describe small plants, including dwarf shrubs, that are suitable for rock gardens

annual a plant that lives and dies in the space of one season and reproduces itself by seed

arboretum a collection of widely different species of trees, sometimes shrubs, grown for botanical interest

biennial a plant that takes two years to come to maturity

bog garden marshy soil that may occur naturally round a stream, but is sometimes artificially made to display marginal plants

bonsai a tree that has been artificially dwarfed for its decorative value. This technique is an ancient one perfected by the Japanese and involves root pruning and restriction

calcifuge a plant or shrub – for example, rhododendron and camellia – that will not grow on a limey soil, only an acid one

climber a plant that grows upwards towards the light, supporting itself by hooks, tendrils, aerial roots, stalks or suction pads

Compositae the daisy family

conifer a tree or shrub like a fir, cedar or pine, that is usually evergreen, tends to have needle-like leaves, and produces its seeds in cones

conservatory a decorative glasshouse, attached to a building, used for keeping delicate or exotic plants

cordon a fruit tree that is trained to grow as a single spur-bearing stem or stems. These may be upright or diagonal

deciduous trees or shrubs that lose their leaves in winter

ericaceous name given to plants of the Ericacae family such as heathers, and also lime-hating plants like rhododendrons

fastigiate description of tree or shrub which has an erect pencil habit of growth; for example, the Lombardy poplar

folly a garden building set there purely for fun, often in the shape of a ruin. Some follies were used to hide something, such as a water tank, or used for some practical purpose – as a look-out, or for keeping doves

glaucous description of grey-blue foliage. Any plant with a name ending with 'glauca' will have leaves of this colouring

grotto an ornamental cave; a popular ingredient of the landscape movement in the 18th century. It usually contained a water feature of some sort and was usually set by a lake

ha-ha a deep-set ditch, invisible from a distance, separating farmland from pleasure grounds and preventing cattle and other livestock from straying into the gardens. The ha-ha was used a great deal in the 18th century, when the landscape movement aimed to make the garden appear to blend in with the land around it

half-hardy name for plants that cannot survive frost and need to be taken indoors during the winter

hardy plants which can normally withstand frost and cold winters

herbaceous technically the name for plants which produce soft rather than woody growth, but also used to describe perennials in general. They usually die back in the autumn and produce fresh shoots from their base in early spring

knot an intricate pattern made with box or some other shrubby small-leaved slow-growing subject, kept close-clipped and filled either with coloured gravel or with other plants. Knots were always laid out so that the pattern could be viewed from a terrace or the upstairs windows of the house. Popular in Elizabethan times, knots have made something of a come-back today

maze a puzzle path designed in an intricate and sometimes symbolic pattern. Originally cut in turf, they were later often edged with clipped box or yew. A maze with high hedges is, strictly speaking, a labyrinth

mount a Tudor invention; an artificially-made mound, designed so that the garden could be viewed from the top of it

154

mulch a top cover of organic material – straw, peat, shredded bark, plastic sheeting etc – which is spread around the roots of plants to help smother weeds, keep moisture in, and in some cases provide nutrients

obelisk a tall decorative structure made from stone or wood. Usually in the shape of an elongated pyramid, it was sometimes used as a memorial to someone or something, but often purely as a decorative focal point

orangery the earliest form of conservatory, built originally to house orange trees during the winter. Later orangeries were used for all sorts of delicate plants

parterre a 17th-century French word for what is essentially a large knot. An openwork, usually geometric pattern, often sited on a terrace, edged in clipped box, brick or stone. Most parterres were filled with coloured gravel and/or plants, but some had water in them instead

parterre de broderie a more decorative, less geometric form of parterre

perennial a plant that goes on from year to year

pleached trees, often fruit trees, trained to form a tunnel or a high 'wall'

pollarding severe cutting back of a tree so that its trunk and the base of its main branches are left, encouraging fresh young growth in the spring

semi-double description of a flower with more than the normal number of petals but not as many as in a full double flower

standard a tree, or sometimes a shrub, that has a bare stem reaching for several feet before the first branches appear. Standard forms of many plants are created by pruning

stew ponds a series of ponds, either natural or man-made, used in medieval monasteries or castles to keep fish until needed for the table

stove house an original name for a greenhouse or conservatory that was heated first with open fires, and later with purpose-built stoves, many of which gave off noxious fumes that in some cases injured the exotic plants growing in these conditions

sub-shrub a plant that falls between a shrub and a herbaceous plant in that it has some woody growth but the green top growth dies back each year. The rose of Sharon (*Hypericum calycinum*) comes into this category

tapestry hedge a hedge that is made from more than one variety of shrub, sometimes purposely mixed, sometimes occurring naturally as in the case of roadside hedges in the country. Botanists claim that it is possible to estimate the age of a hedge by the number of different shrubs in it

topiary the art of clipping trees or shrubs into unnatural shapes. Known since ancient Roman times, the fashion was revived by André Le Nôtre in the 17th century. It became popular again in Victorian England

treillage an elaborate decoration or structure made from wood (or sometimes metal) trellis. It could be an obelisk, an arch or simply placed against a wall

trompe-l'oeil meaning literally 'deceiving the eye' in French, this is the skill of creating an illusion in the garden, or in the house, using mirrors, painted façades, false perspective trellis arranged so that although flat against the wall it appears to be a tunnel. It is also used in landscaping – for example, making a path narrow towards the far end so that it looks longer than it actually is

vista an artificially created view of the countryside beyond a garden, made either by planting an avenue of trees to point to it, or sometimes a grass path or a canal

wilderness a carefully laid out woodland area, usually planted to contrast with the formal gardens around a house. It is the antecedent of the Victorian shrubbery

Index

———◆———

159

Acknowledgements

———◆———

The photographs were supplied by the photographers and agencies listed below:

AA Photolibrary pp. 2, 43, 67, 87, 89, 136
Jeffrey Beazley pp. 37, 92, 111
John Bethell pp. 12–13, 15, 18, 23, 25, 28–9, 31, 40, 46, 48–9, 53, 56–7, 64, 69,
72, 74, 82–3, 85, 94, 100, 108–9, 113, 116, 119, 120
Marianne Majerus pp. 97, 134
National Trust Photographic Library/Nick Carter p. 81; Eric Crichton p. 141;
Jerry Harpur p. 143; Andrew Lawson p. 105; Rob Matheson p. 129; Nick Meers
pp. 8, 123, 138; Derry Moore p. 124 (and front cover); David Noton p. 34;
Ian Shaw p. 131; Mike Williams pp. 6, 62
Robert O'Dea pp. 77, 99, 103

The line drawings are by Lyn Cawley, and the garden illustrations in the
gazetteer are by Sheilagh Noble.

The maps on pp. 58–61 were drawn by John Gilkes.